Help!
My Kids Don't All Speak
English

Help!
My Kids Don't All Speak
English

How to Set Up a Language Workshop
in Your Linguistically Diverse Classroom

Nancy Akhavan
Foreword by ELAINE M. GARAN

Heinemann
Portsmouth, NH

Heinemann
A division of Reed Elsevier Inc.
361 Hanover Street
Portsmouth, NH 03801–3912
www.heinemann.com

Offices and agents throughout the world

Library of Congress Cataloging-in-Publication Data
Akhavan, Nancy L.
  Help! my kids don't all speak English : how to set up a language workshop in your linguistically diverse classroom / Nancy L. Akhavan ; foreword by Elaine M. Garan.
      p. cm.
  Includes bibliographical references and index.
  ISBN 0-325-00798-5 (alk. paper)
    1. English language—Study and teaching—Foreign speakers.
  2. English language—Study and teaching—Foreign speakers.   3. Limited English proficient students—Education—United States.   I. Title.

PE1128 .A2A34 2006
428 . 0071'2—dc22   2005025912

Editor: Lois Bridges
Production: Lynne Costa
Cover design: Jenny Jensen Greenleaf
Cover photograph: Nancy Akhavan
Typesetter: Publishers' Design and Production Services, Inc.
Manufacturing: Steve Bernier

Printed in the United States of America on acid-free paper

09 08 07 06   VP   2 3 4 5

For Mehran,
who shared with me the joy of two languages

Contents

APPENDIXES

Foreword

Nancy Akhavan is a builder of bridges. Thousands of teachers and administrators have read and been transformed by her first book, *How to Align Literacy Instruction, Assessment, and Standards*. In it she showed us how she helped a faltering, low-performing school evolve into a joyful, academically successful community of learners. In that book, Nancy built a bridge between the "musts" of standards and mandates and meaningful instruction for students.

In this, her second book, *Help! My Kids Don't All Speak English*, Nancy again draws on her own rich experience as a bilingual and primary teacher—and as an administrator in schools educating large numbers of multilingual children—to help teachers meet the challenges of working with linguistically diverse students. Here again, Nancy builds a bridge. She helps teachers infuse standards and mandates into classrooms that offer rich, motivating language experiences for those students who need it most. After reading this book, teachers will be inspired to structure their own workshops to honor the unique cultures and languages of students. And they will have the tools to do so without sacrificing the direct, focused instruction of basic skills required by state and district mandates.

Nancy herself has experienced what many teachers today are facing as they find themselves "drowning" with extra duties, to say nothing of the stress and added challenge of ensuring that English learners meet target performance standards. Nancy has been there, has experienced those frustrations, has made mistakes and learned from them, and now she has a wealth of practical knowledge to help teachers and administrators negotiate these challenges.

Her insights and experiences are woven throughout her new book. Nancy knows that strong language workshops don't just happen—they occur by design. While many teachers are intrigued by and would love to implement a workshop approach, some are hesitant to do so because they are not sure how to get started. They fear the loss of control they may associate with classrooms that encourage student talk, debate, and peer interactions. And they fear the loss of focused instruction that they believe will help students meet standards and mandates and raise test scores.

Nancy assuages those fears. She takes readers by the hand and guides them through every aspect of creating a workshop. Beginning at square one, Nancy explains how to manage every detail right down to how we can best display books and materials. Nancy reminds us of the stages of language acquisition and offers us activities and vivid examples from her own experience so that we can bridge the gap between the theoretical and the practical. She gives us examples of student work and vivid descriptions of teachers and students interacting in a language workshop setting. To do so, she draws upon her own vast experience as a teacher as well as insight she has gained from the hundreds of classrooms she has visited.

Nancy also provides checklists for teachers and students alike so that assessment helps us target specific student needs. Assessment, then, becomes an integral and meaningful part of the language workshop approach that informs our instruction *and* provides a structure that keeps us focused.

Through her detailed descriptions, Nancy shows us how to support students so they do not simply acquire language at a surface level, but learn to use it to think, debate, and problem solve. As Nancy reminds us, sadly, these deeper, richer layers of language usage are too often ignored in more traditional, skills-based settings where many bilingual children and linguistically diverse students often receive a watered-down curriculum, one that is heavy on isolated skills and sparse in opportunities to use real language for authentic purposes.

The chapter on vocabulary development alone will change classrooms. Here, Nancy offers a wealth of practical ideas and tackles the challenge that so many of us face: How do we teach vocabulary so that it goes beyond free-floating, rote definitions to richer, grounded, more valuable instruction that resonates and truly connects to students' lives? And, how do we do that and still structure our teaching so that it is direct and precise? Nancy shows us how.

I am a professor of teacher education in an area that has a large population of linguistically and ethnically diverse students. Teachers in our area as well as the preservice teachers in our courses do not want theory alone; they want answers. They want practical ideas on how to implement those abstract theories. I believe that is partly why I was so taken with this book. There is nothing abstract or purely theoretical about it. It connects the dots between the *why* and the down-to-earth *how* of meeting the challenges so many of us face in linguistically diverse classrooms.

Finally, this is a refreshingly readable book. As I read it, I lingered over pages. It was as if I were sitting down with a good friend and teacher who was willing to share her experiences with me. Nancy Akhavan offers us a work that is at once wise and compassionate, precise and practical. This is a book that honors the uniqueness of students and teachers alike. It is a book that will leave readers feeling renewed and fully prepared to create classrooms that resound with the joy of language.

Elaine M. Garan
Associate Professor in the Department
of Literacy and Early Education
California State University, Fresno

Acknowledgments

This book has a history; like teachers who gather together in the lounge or the parking lot to tell the tales of the latest happenings in their classrooms, this book has a story. It begins with the wonderful teachers with whom I have worked over many years: from sharing a rushed lunch in a classroom before the bell rang, to challenging ideas and pondering questions in staff development workshops, to conferring over an important piece of student work. I thank all of you who have touched my work. I have learned much.

I would especially like to acknowledge the teachers who celebrate the rich diversity they find in their classrooms. Shana Simpson, whose careful reflection and incredible lessons go far beyond her years experience, has opened my eyes to how far young children can go when they have support from a fabulous teacher. If not for Kristina Karlson's perseverance and commitment to teaching multilingual children and children of poverty, I wouldn't have tried many of the lessons you will find in the pages of this book. Kim León's leadership and knowledge of literacy practices helped design the planning and intensity of the language workshop. Two of the most passionate teachers I know are Sharon Mayo and Andrea Ermie. Sharon, an outstanding teacher, combined her passion for justice with literacy practices to teach children in powerful and meaningful ways. Andrea leads an outstanding curriculum that encourages students to ponder and question; it was in Andrea's classroom where I learned to debate books while sitting on the floor with fourth graders.

Most recently I have had the honor of serving as principal at Pinedale Elementary School in Fresno, California. The team of teachers at Pinedale are committed to teaching the students of diverse backgrounds who come to school faithfully every day. A group of teachers at Pinedale who sprung into action the first year I worked with them met the needs of their culturally and linguistically diverse students through focused and powerful literacy instruction. All of them had the faith to delve into a curriculum that draws on student strengths and to teach lessons that make children think through sustained literacy practices. I would also like to thank all the staff members at Pinedale who contributed to the ideas in this book; in particular Gloria Alvarez, Michele Hart, Anissa Daniel, Lori Garcia-Higgs, Pam Pflepsen, Hollie Olsen, Shelley Vizcarra, Laurie Cruz, Patti Moore, Susan Harper, and Kristen Belknap.

The work presented in this book grew and developed from a community of learners beyond the classrooms in California. I would also like to thank Joann Wilson-Keenan, principal of Mary O. Pottenger School in Massachusetts, and her teachers. Many of the lessons in this book were developed for students at her school. Pottenger School is a very special school filled with books, children hungry to read and learn, and a dynamic staff. Their commitment to excellence and focus on literacy and language shine in the halls of their building. I would especially like to thank Kathy Adonis, a wonderful teacher with an incredible second-grade classroom, for helping with student permissions.

This book exists only because of the commitment of the staff at Heinemann. Leigh Peake's focus on providing high-quality, powerful, and sustainable professional development to teachers across the nation nurtures the teachers who are learning and the authors who are creating. Thank you for your focus and belief that a professional learning community is most important to excellence in education. I appreciate your support. I have also had the pleasure of working with Lynne Costa, who championed the production process of my first book. Thank you. And most of all, thank you to my editor, Lois Bridges. This book is complete because of her focus and her commitment to teachers and children. To Lois, a book is an opportunity for all educators to learn and grow, and she supported my writing in numerous ways in order to move this project from manuscript to published book. Her commitment, drive, and passion are immeasurable, and she has a profound effect on education as she tirelessly reads manuscripts and gives careful feedback.

Last, I would like to thank my husband and children, who always stand beside me, waiting for me to finish a book so that we can celebrate together. I love all of you so, and I could not write even one word if you weren't part of the journey.

Teach students to think about ideas, information, issues, and things that matter, teach them how to speak, listen, and write about these things, and if you do . . . they will hold the world in their hands.

PART ONE

Preparing for Language Instruction

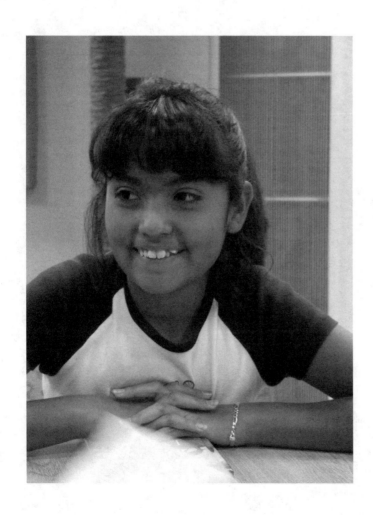

CHAPTER ONE

Teaching Language

Language. It is the medium we use to hold our lives together, to communicate, to learn, to hope, to think, to love. Glance at a classroom filled with children (perhaps your classroom), and you will hear and see language used in many different ways: children are laughing, talking, reading, writing, thinking, and conversing with the teacher. Glance at the classroom again after the children have gone home, and you will see language at use in many silent, but influential ways: charts, recorded ideas, daily agendas, books, lists of information, intriguing quotes, word walls. While I write this I am sitting in the sixth-grade classroom of Louanne Brunolli at Nelson Elementary School in Fresno, California; here I sit awash in language. There is an array of children around me using language for various purposes:

- talking
- conferring
- listening
- reading
- writing
- reporting
- investigating
- thinking
- recording
- exploring

I also see children with varying language needs in Louanne's classroom. The children include

- English learners
- fluent English-proficient students (students no longer designated as English learners)
- native English speakers

- speakers of other languages from at least three different countries
- students who speak English as a first language with varying abilities in academic language and formal discourse
- engaged learners focused on their work

Most importantly, in Louanne's room I see children. Her room is full of individual children with individual needs. They are learning to add depth to their vocabularies by focusing on powerful phrases and ideas related to academic genres. In contrast, I don't see a group to lament over or quantify in numbers based on their test scores. I see children who need a very skilled teacher to help them learn everything they need to know in order to succeed in school and in life. This begins with becoming a language teacher. Language makes our world revolve, helps us connect with each other and communicate up close and from afar. There are classrooms that celebrate language, develop language, and infuse their space with language. There are classrooms where language and thought hang in the air and become tangible when one enters the room and spots the books, poems, thoughts, quotes, beautiful words, newspapers, intriguing facts, and historical issues that fill the shelves, brighten the walls, and line the countertops. Language is everywhere. Language is the soul of these classrooms; without it the air would become stale and the classroom atmosphere would be much less rich. This is the type of classroom and community you can build with your students.

This book is designed to show you how to create a language classroom that meets the needs of the English learners as they acquire English, as well as the needs of linguistically diverse students who speak English as a first language but require language development. Specifically, this book will show you how to organize and teach a block of time dedicated to language use and acquisition in a workshop format.

Teaching the Language Workshop

I have spent more than sixteen years teaching in California schools. During this time I have worked as a bilingual teacher in a late-exit bilingual program, as a primary teacher certified to teach language in a nonbilingual program, and as an administrator of programs and schools educating large numbers of linguistically diverse children. I have seen a lot of change in California regarding the teaching of English to children who speak other languages. Current legislation in California and the No Child Left Behind Act mandate accountability measures and growth in standardized test scores that measure English acquisition. The pressure to perform can lead teachers away from best practices in teaching language in the hopes of meeting a mandate (Garan 2004).

But there is another way to face the pressure of legislation and test scores: focus on the child, and create a classroom environment where children learn language naturally in a workshop setting. When teaching language in a workshop, it is possible to incorporate all of the school or district expectations you face with good pedagogical practices that are supported by research and years of experience by experts in the field. Workshop teaching leads you back to the child, and what each child needs to learn in order to succeed in school, while you facilitate learning, promote cognitive growth, create motivation from within each child, and celebrate student successes in a supportive, nurturing environment.

In a workshop, learning is

- Constructed by the children
- Facilitated by the teacher
- Organized in units of study around socially important ideas, comprehension strategies, or genres
- Natural and occurs for each child in individual ways
- Shared between children through peer groups and partnerships
- Collective between the whole class, groups, and the teacher
- Cooperative—no one is seen as holding all knowledge, including the teacher

In a workshop, children are

- Active—they move about the classroom
- Responsible for their learning, thinking, reading, and writing
- Motivated to participate in reading, writing, and discussion around topics of interest
- Nurtured by the teacher to learn specific strategies, to have ideas, and to learn to speak, listen, read, and write well
- Learning constantly

In a workshop, teachers are

- Designing units of study based on standards and student needs
- Participating in discussions, reading groups, and writing
- Facilitating learning
- Creating visuals such as charts and manipulatives to support learning
- Immersing children in language through story, poetry, nonfiction studies, music, and discussion
- Teaching precisely language, strategies, and information so that children own the learning and have responsibility for the knowledge
- Assessing through anecdotal notes, running records, kidwatching, and teacher-made assessments in order to determine and teach to each child's needs

Before thinking about starting a language workshop in your classroom, let's consider a broader picture: what language instruction looks like throughout the day.

CHAPTER TWO

Traits of Language Classrooms

Under the tree at recess, Mrs. Rios, a parent, stands in the shade. She stands with her daughter and a bunch of her little friends. They all bob around Mrs. Rios' feet like bubbles coming to the water's surface. Their faces are shining as they talk in rapid Spanish about everything that they did over the weekend. They smile at her with chocolate eyes and dimpled cheeks. I ask, "¿Senora, como está?" I go on to ask about her weekend and her family. She responds and the words come out in a joyful rush. Partway through the conversation, I realize that I have stopped listening. I cannot grasp each word.

I wonder how often my students stop listening. When? At which phrase do they tune out? Is it at the beginning of my lesson, in the middle, or at the end, right before I say the most important thing? The truth is I need to tell the most important information first and then develop their understanding to help them grasp the idea. Children learning English need repeated exposure to meaningful language. They also need support and acceptance of their native language.

Effective teaching strategies are critical to the success of linguistically and culturally diverse students. After working with many, many teachers who taught English learners over the years, I've noticed seven attributes that appear over and over again in effective classrooms. These seven attributes reflect the core beliefs of the teachers and also are grounded in research and literature regarding the acquisition of English. While these core beliefs don't encompass everything that occurs in a classroom, or in the design of effective instruction for linguistically and culturally diverse students, they provide a framework for the implementation of a language workshop.

Core Beliefs of a Language Classroom

1. Children acquire English by engaging in language in a meaningful context in their own way and at their own pace. Language acquisition

follows an accepted path arranged loosely in five stages: preproduction, early production, speech emergence, intermediate fluency, and advanced fluency.

2. Quality conversations lead to thinking and learning across the curriculum and about issues in our lives and world. Language teachers focus on content and language at the same time and plan for talk and learning in various discourses.

3. Learners need frequent, sustained time to speak, listen, read, and write each day in order to acquire language and engage with content.

4. A child's home language and culture should be an integral part of her learning and cognitive development. In language classrooms this diversity is celebrated through literature, literary nonfiction, poetry, and music. This practice creates an underlying support structure for all students. Their language and cultural backgrounds are supported and respected.

5. Children construct knowledge through precise and authentic instruction when supported by carefully designed atmospheres that engage, nurture, and challenge.

6. Children must be exposed to a large quantity of print in several genres. The print should be an integral part of the classroom and school atmosphere. A range of print includes fiction, nonfiction, literature, literary nonfiction, multimedia print, and environmental print.

7. Linguistically diverse children learn best in cooperative communities where learning and ideas are shared to ensure that all students engage and are respected. Children are part of the classroom community, and the students are not expected to learn in isolation.

A Glimpse at Two Language Classrooms

Middle School Writing Workshop

Taryn Harmon opens the book *The Tin Forest* (Ward 2001) while she stands in front of her seventh-grade students. She holds it up for all of them to see. "I like this book and I want to share it with you because in the book the author uses description to make the world believable. I can see the make-believe world she creates when I read the words."

Taryn walks over to her easel, where she has written, "Ways authors help us believe the context of their writing." She adds this sentence: "I can see this imaginary world in my mind when the author describes the setting." Taryn says, "Do all of you remember this page when I read the book yesterday? I think the words are beautiful, but more importantly they help me see this make-believe world." Then she continues, "I think this writing is powerful because I can imagine the world while I am reading because of the details the author uses. I highlighted those details here on the photocopy of page 12 that I put on the chart. I put this here so you can remind yourselves how the author, Helen Ward, crafted her story so that we can see the context."

"I want you to try this today in your writing. Look at your drafts of the character you are writing about who was alive during the Civil War. Is your context clear to the reader? Is it engaging? Authentic? Think of ways you can add details. Yesterday, I conferred with Juan. He was stuck because he had only written a couple of short sentences about where his character had lost his leg in the war. When I read his piece, I wasn't sure where this life-changing event occurred. Juan explained to me that it happened on the character's property when he was fighting thieves and beggars, but I just couldn't see that in my mind." Taryn flips the switch on the overhead projector. "I copied his writing onto the overhead. Let's see if we can give Juan some coaching advice. I want to help him slow down his writing and make it rich with details so that I can imagine the context. Come on up here and join me, Juan."

Juan goes to the front of the class and sits on a tall stool next to the overhead projector. Taryn stands next to him and they talk through his piece. When Taryn questions him to explain in greater details, he describes his thinking. Taryn adds some of his thoughts in the margin. At the end of the lesson Taryn points out how the students can revise the beginning of their piece to put more details in the context. She points to a basket of picture books that have good descriptions of setting and character feelings and actions. She invites the class to use the picture books (which the students have previously read) as a guide to help them craft details as they continue to work on writing a historical fiction piece.

Elementary School Reading Workshop Minilesson
Shana Simpson gathers her class on the rug in the corner of her classroom. Everywhere around her are books and charts dripping with language—about things the class has discussed together, favorite words, big ideas, and so on. She settles into her chair with the children nestled at her feet. "Today, first graders, we are going to write in a new genre. I love this genre because I always learn so many new things when I read. This book," she says, holding up a leveled-text book from her collection titled *Tiger* (Whitehouse 2003), "is nonfiction. We have been reading lots of nonfiction out loud in our class to prepare us to write a nonfiction report and to help us learn to understand new ideas and information when we read. Guess what we are going to do right now? We are going on a nonfiction hunt. When I say *go*, I want you to go around the classroom and bring back anything in the classroom that you think might be nonfiction."

One of the children raises his hand. "Will it be in a book?"

"Maybe, but you might find nonfiction writing in our classroom that is not in a book. I want you to go on your nonfiction search with your writing partner. So look at the book in my hands one more time, and then find your partner and go!"

As soon as Shana says *go*, the children stand and partner up; then they spread out around the classroom. Maria and Jessica are paired together;

they are both English learners and began kindergarten speaking only Spanish. As they walk around the room together, they converse in Spanish, occasionally looking back at the book Shana has displayed. Jessica picks up a book in the classroom library and opens the front cover. The book has a table of contents. The girls talk in Spanish and then Maria nods her head vigorously and the girls decide to take the book back to the teacher.

"Great job, first graders," Shana tells the children as they come back to the rug. "Now, sit on the rug with your partner and look at your book together. I want you to tell us what you like about the book, or other item you have brought, and tell us why you think it is nonfiction."

As Shana moves about the circle, the children take turns sharing. One partner holds up the item and the other partner shares with the class why they think it is an example of nonfiction. Some children point to pictures or the index. Shana writes all of their ideas on a chart that is titled "Features of Nonfiction Text." Maria responds in Spanish when it is her turn to share; then her partner explains Maria's thoughts in English. Shana records Maria's contribution to the chart in English because she is not bilingual.

Carefully Constructed Learning

Both Shana's classroom and Taryn's classroom are language classrooms. There are features in both classrooms that support literacy development for students from diverse language backgrounds, including those who are learning English. Both Taryn and Shana show children what they want them to do and record their ideas and then coach them to think and to revise their work as needed.

Shana's and Taryn's classrooms include features that support literacy and language learning and stem from the core beliefs that these teachers hold about how linguistically and culturally diverse students learn language (Darling-Hammond 1997; Freeman and Freeman 1998; Herrera and Murray 2005; Rothstein-Fisch, Greenfield, and Trumbull 1999). These are just some of those features:

- Language is taught through content.
- Concrete examples are modeled.
- Students use mentor texts as guides to acquiring language and improving writing.
- Collaborative learning is supported by having students work in pairs to think and engage in an activity.
- Community is developed as a fundamental component of instruction.
- Students are allowed to use their primary language in order to communicate and develop understanding of content.
- Reading, writing, listening, and speaking are developed in each lesson.
- A supportive context for learning English is developed, emphasizing the needs of all students to improve their reading and writing abilities.

- Teachers emphasize active, in-depth learning by focusing students on doing purposeful work that approximates the work of real writers and critics.
- Teachers emphasize authentic performances.

Developing Classroom Culture: Step Inside a Language Classroom

Like Taryn's and Shana's classrooms, wonderful classrooms occur by design. There are several things teachers need to consider when developing their classrooms. It is easiest to think of these important features by considering three major traits of authentic, collaborative language classrooms. (See Figure 2.1.)

The first trait is *context*. Context creates a frame of reference for the teacher to use when designing a classroom, including materials and how the physical arrangement of the room affects student learning. The context also includes student needs. Assessment guides effective instruction, and assessment shows us where to begin teaching a child. In this context, when we pay close attention, we can motivate students, better meet their needs, and feel more effective as teachers. Context also includes teaching. Think of this as the manner in which we choose to deliver content. Specific instructional content drives our choices as educators. Many teachers instruct through workshops, believe that learning to read is a psycholinguistic process, teach writing through authentic and purposeful investigations, and teach language by focusing on communication and comprehensible mes-

FIGURE 2.1 Three Traits of Collaborative Language Classroom

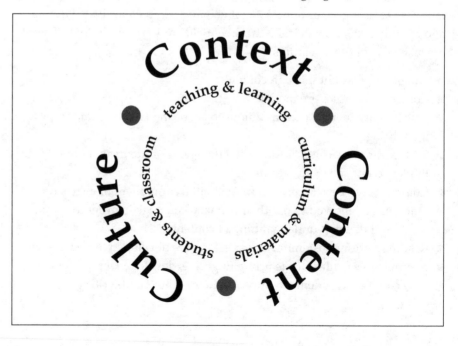

sages. These are contexts for teaching and learning; they provide better learning opportunities for culturally and linguistically diverse students (Towle 2000). *Context includes teaching, students' academic needs, and classroom design.*

The second trait is *culture*. The students' backgrounds and cultures provide rich resources for the teacher in the design of a language classroom. Student culture includes how students perceive issues and information, their native languages, their rituals and traditions, and the unique perspectives students bring to the classroom. Culture also refers to the classroom. Each classroom has a culture, and it is best if the teacher can specifically design the culture that is desired. Classroom culture includes how students interact, the teacher's philosophy of education, the school's rules and expectations, and how the teacher designs the classroom to work. Students from minority backgrounds often bring collective values to the classroom. Collectivism focuses on the good of the group rather than the success of individuals. Collectivism emphasizes the social context of learning and knowledge (Rothstein-Fisch, Greenfield, and Trumbull 1999). This is one reason collaborative work supports and nurtures culturally and linguistically diverse students. The culture of the students and the culture of the classroom have an indelible impression on learning. *Culture includes student backgrounds and classroom culture.*

The third trait is *content*. Content includes the content of the curriculum and the content of instruction. There is content to the curriculum we teach. This curriculum is often driven by state standards, national guidelines, and the scope of series adoptions and sequence manuals. It is also driven by teacher knowledge and expertise about language and literacy learning. There is also content to the materials. What we choose to use in our rooms to teach from, for students to read, to use as models, and to use as environmental print all has content. The content of these materials should validate students' languages and backgrounds, facilitate learning, and provide a bridge between students' understanding, their motivation, and our pedagogical choices. The best classrooms are full of literature and literary nonfiction texts that reflect the plurality of the classroom, the school, and the greater community around the school (Nathenson-Mejia and Escamilla 2003). *Content includes curriculum and materials.*

These three traits—context, content, and culture—encompass the core beliefs that Shana and Taryn believe in and apply in their classrooms. They pay close attention to each trait, because if their classrooms were missing the essential components of one of the traits, the atmosphere, the learning, and the delivery of instruction would be less effective. By carefully implementing instruction around the traits and designing classrooms to support learning in authentic and meaningful ways, Taryn and Shana are creating appropriate and effective learning opportunities for students.

It is important to think about how language is used to communicate, teach, respond, and reflect. Shana and Taryn work hard to create a particular atmosphere in which children are supported and nurtured, but most importantly that when you open their classroom doors and walk inside you are dazzled by the atmosphere in the classroom. There is no doubt in these classrooms that literacy, language, and thinking are most valued and that the child builds knowledge through exposure, playfulness, joy, authentic work, rigorous expectations, and an immersion in language and literature. You can implement these same ideas in your classroom. Begin by considering each trait and thinking about how these traits are implemented in your room.

PART TWO

Language Learning

CHAPTER THREE

The Language Workshop

Christine sat in the comfortable armchair in the meeting area in her room. Her fifth-grade students had gathered on the floor in front of her. Beside her was an easel with a thick pad of chart paper, and on the floor at her feet were baskets and baskets of books. As she read, she would pause often and ask, "What are you thinking? Do you have any ideas about how the character is feeling now?"

Mila, who just finished conferring with her partner, shot her hand up. "Oh, I think she feels depressed!"

"*Depressed*, wow! That is a great word. Tell us why you think Lara feels depressed," Christine replied.

Mila hesitated for a moment. "Well, where she lives, it is different than home, and that man ["Her uncle," Mila's partner, Sienna, piped in], yeah, her *uncle*, well, he is really busy and Lara misses her family. So I think she is depressed." Christine quickly recorded Mila's thinking on the chart paper and then called on another student to share.

Asking children to think about characters' thoughts and feelings isn't new, and narrowing in on Mila's use of the word *depressed* isn't exceptional in a classroom where children have lots of experience talking, but what made this lesson different was that the students were English learners and Mila was not proficient in English. Before Christine began teaching fifth grade at a school made up of mostly minority students from diverse language backgrounds, and where the majority of the children lived in poverty, she was asked in her interview, "Now, there are many English learners here. What experiences do you have in teaching English learners?"

Christine stammered while answering that she had very little experience with English learners but she thought that if she just exposed them to English, everything would be fine. Her teaching experience had been in schools with one or two English learners in each class, and there wasn't a distinction between English learners and linguistically diverse students who were developing language skills. In the beginning of her first year, Christine focused on surviving her first few months in the classroom, but in the spring she knew that she needed to make changes to her day. Most of her students were not developing as much English as she felt they could. Christine decided to set aside the mechanical structures of language instruction that were included in the program that the school had purchased to teach language, and she redesigned her daily agenda and classroom structure to include a language workshop. Christine was not disappointed in the progress that her students made in learning language in this new structure. In addition, she felt confident and positive about her teaching.

Looking at Instruction: Goals for Language Workshop

For several years as a specially certificated language teacher, I taught English learners and linguistically diverse students. I also taught as a bilingual teacher providing primary language instruction in Spanish. During these years I struggled to effectively implement content-based English language development (ELD) or English as a second language (ESL) for a minimum of thirty minutes (the state requirement) in an authentic and engaging way. I knew from extended study at Fresno Pacific University under professors Yvonne and David Freeman that English learners acquire language best when they have instruction that is

- Authentic (when students read, write, and talk for extended periods of time)
- Focused on student needs
- Based on content grouped in themes
- Supported with visual aids
- Scaffolded with graphic organizers
- Sheltered (special considerations are made for English learners, including using visuals, slowing speech, and providing cooperative learning opportunities)
- Grounded in content
- Tied to reading and writing development (Freeman and Freeman, 1998).

I also worked as a specialist in English language development outside of the classroom for several years. I wanted ELD to be as authentic and engaging as possible and linked to units of study in reading and writing workshops. But the best way to implement effective, authentic, engaging language instruction was not apparent. I could provide a lot of literacy instruction to my English learners and linguistically diverse students in reading and writing workshops, but there was an element missing. I was not supporting English learners in the three dimensions of language development (see Chapter 4 for more information):

- Conversational fluency—ability to carry on face-to-face conversations
- Discrete language skills—specific phonological, literacy, and grammatical knowledge taught in context
- Academic language proficiency—knowledge of less frequent vocabulary and the ability to interpret and produce increasingly complex language

In particular, I was not increasing their skills in conversation around academic content. Learning content is not enough; students have to be able to discuss their ideas in groups, argue their points, and support their ideas with evidence. After working with many teachers in kindergarten through grade 6, I found this to be true in many classrooms. Half an hour devoted to language learning was focused on conversation skills, academic language, and discrete skills, but the mode of instruction included artificial and contrived activities. The mainstream English learners were getting ahead of the linguistically diverse students because they came to school with the language, were given more opportunities to think, debate, and defend ideas, and were given powerful and authentic instruction. Overall linguistically diverse students were involved in unpurposeful instruction. They would sit quietly, doing worksheets, answering a multitude of questions after reading, or reading books that were too difficult and not at their instructional or independent level. Sometimes they were lost in a workshop setting because they didn't have the same language abilities as their peers. In addition, in the classrooms of many teachers I worked with, the students would be on grade level, and perhaps reclassified from English learner to fluent English speaker in third grade, only to struggle in fourth, fifth, and sixth grade (Chall and Jacobs 2003). The main reason for the struggle was that the students had not developed academic language proficiency; that is, they did not know how to discuss their ideas in groups, or how to support their ideas with information, and they also did not know how to connect to and think through texts. This is a common problem (Delpit 1989).

Context of Education

Another pervasive problem is the context within which we teach. Chapter 2 discusses how our instruction occurs within a context. This context is affected by factors outside of our classroom. As educators we are at a very special moment in time; there are four main factors currently influencing the focus of classrooms.

1. The No Child Left Behind Act of 2001, signed into law in early 2002, the most sweeping federal school reform legislation in history, mandates proficiency on high-stakes exams and places pressure to improve student performance on schools filled with children from diverse backgrounds (Tucker and Toch 2004).
2. Twenty-five years of research in reading comprehension provides insight and direction to reading instruction, and as the art of teaching

shares the stage with the science of teaching, we have available a large amount of information to help us design classrooms where all children can learn to read and write well (Allington and Cunningham 2001; Pressley 2002; Marzano 2003).

3. The demographics of the United States are changing rapidly. Freeman and Freeman (2003) state that in the last decade, not only did the number of English learners double from 2 million to 4.3 million, but there was also an increase in the variety of languages represented by students entering school. Census Bureau projections show that the population of children learning English will continue to grow. Children who are learning English will constitute an estimated 40 percent of the school-age population in the United States by the year 2030 and children who speak a nonstandard form of English continue to need language development (Shin and Brun 2003; Delpit and Dowdy 2002).

4. The achievement gap between minority students and white students persists; the equal access sought in schools for several decades has not led to equal achievement (Barton 2004; Rumberger and Anguiano 2004). Many culturally and linguistically diverse students leave elementary school not fully literate and not achieving grade level expectations (Gutiérrez 2001; Haycock 2001a, 2001b). To address the achievement gap, educators use online resources and technology in the classroom to track data, communicate, plan, and design instruction (Winn 2004; Vang 2004).

It is not easy to embrace the sweeping changes that we find at our schoolhouse doors. To effectively create and sustain student achievement in our schools filled with children learning English, and children who have historically scored low on high-stakes exams, we have to be careful and thoughtful in planning our classrooms, the delivery of curriculum, and the effectiveness of instruction. It is no longer enough to teach as we have always taught, or to limit our own learning and be expected to use only a scripted series to teach reading and language. It is equally not enough to *not* systematically plan for the needs of English learners. We have to create powerful classrooms where children have the best chance to succeed. Your students can learn to read and think while still learning English; English-speaking students can learn the differences between their maternal dialect and academic language in ways that validate and motivate them (Goldenberg 2001). We have to plan well in order to implement something new.

We need to show children how to interact with each other, think about ideas that extend their understanding of issues and texts beyond recall, and connect these experiences to reading. We can effectively scaffold instruction so that English learners and linguistically diverse students have experiences with talking and thinking in academic settings with content information. To meet the needs of students I recommend carving thirty minutes out of your instructional day to add a third workshop—language workshop.

What Language Workshop Is

The premise of the language workshop is that language is acquired through shared discussions while thinking about books (both fiction and nonfiction), processing information, and posing questions for learning. The teacher creates an atmosphere where shared discussion (including teacher to student, student to student, and student to teacher) is natural and needed for the classroom to function well and for the children to learn (Akhavan 2004).

Language workshop is simply language development taught in a workshop setting. This gives English learners and linguistically diverse students a special time focused on the specific language needs they have. Children then have guidance and opportunity to acquire language, learn structures of discussion and debate, and learn structures for thinking through ideas and texts. The workshop gives the teacher time to scaffold the learning by posing problems and ideas, teaching specific thinking strategies, and modeling specific uses of language. Children think, reason, and discuss together before they are expected to do the thinking independently.

The scaffolded group practice supports students whose backgrounds nurture a collectivist viewpoint versus individualism. These students come from families who value projects and success that involve many members of the group. Students develop literacy, thinking, and speaking skills in English while developing these same skills in their first language through the group work. When students work in groups, they can use their first language to think and communicate (Haritos 2003). When memory develops in two languages, bilingual students' understanding of skills, processes, concepts, and content is enhanced (Franklin 2004). Since the workshop focuses on modeling discussion and thinking around theme-based concepts, the construction of meaning is enhanced and supported (Avalos 2003; Genesee 1994).

Children Construct Knowledge in Transformative Classrooms

Transformative teaching encourages students to construct meaning, to be part of the learning process, and also to be sources of information and knowledge in the classroom. Transformative teaching encourages teachers to stop standing in front of children, telling them what to do and how to think, and instead move to the side, where they can coach children, facilitate learning, and grow as professional educators (Kohn 1999). This pedagogical approach accommodates different styles of student learning and connection. Vang (2003) states that transformative instruction integrates domain knowledge of various contexts, builds practice into the daily classroom routines, and encourages the transfer of prior learning to new ideas and situations in English and in the students' first language. Vang recommends that interactive, constructivist lessons contain these seven elements:

- expectation
- engagement
- exploration
- explanation
- elaboration
- experience
- evaluation.

In a transformative classroom, the teacher may begin a lesson up front, giving students information, but then he builds in a time for students to interact with the information. Perhaps they write, or talk. The children take the information in by hooking the new knowledge to other information in their brains. They transform what they know by adding new information to their schemata. These processes encourage language acquisition.

Language Development

Oral and written language development is critical to a student's overall development. An English learner needs to develop oral skills in social and academic discourses and needs specific help to acquire language in both discourses. In language workshop students are given a purpose for talking because of the need to share ideas, ask good questions, and discuss information with partners. They are also given the opportunity to respond to texts and write about their thinking.

Goals of language workshop include developing students' ability to

- Make decisions about important themes and ideas in texts they hear read aloud, and in texts they read independently, based on evidence in the text as well as their experiences, knowledge, and beliefs
- Share their ideas, decisions, and beliefs orally and in writing
- Carry on conversations with others about their ideas
- Think critically by analyzing, synthesizing, comparing, and evaluating texts, ideas, and problems
- Think critically by responding orally and in writing with peers and their teacher
- Reason through ideas, texts, and issues
- Think, reason, and discuss together before they are expected to do the thinking independently (Teaching and supporting students through explicit instruction fosters their development.)
- Know and apply proper forms and function of English from modeling
- Acquire language through authentic thinking and speaking opportunities

Language workshop consists of two types of lessons: spontaneous language lessons and scaffolded oral expression lessons (Miramontes, Nadeau, and Commins 1997). While these seem like ambiguous terms, it is important to wrap your mind around the difference between the two types of lessons. The more often you are purposeful in the type of lesson you present, and understand what the lesson is designed to teach, the more your students will learn. You might think, "What does it matter? They are both language lessons!" But there is a clear difference between them.

To make it easier to distinguish between them, I think of them as process lessons and structure lessons.

- Sometimes I am teaching the processes of thinking, speaking, reading, and writing (spontaneous language lessons) and know that students will acquire language while engaged in authentic activities.
- During other lessons I might teach vocabulary, correct forms for writing, or text structures. These are structure lessons, and if taught while applying learning to authentic activities in a workshop, children will acquire language instead of memorizing facts and rules that they may later forget or may not be ready to learn.

Characteristics of Spontaneous Language Lessons (process lessons)

- Use concepts from content areas to increase students' ability to talk about main ideas or interrelated ideas.
- Do not teach new language; instead, the discussion relies upon students' current language abilities.
- Facilitate spontaneous language acquisition through interaction.

Characteristics of Scaffolded Expression Lessons (structure lessons)

- Teach new language structures and vocabulary.
- Teach how to express ideas using new vocabulary or terms in a safe setting.
- Teach form and content with authentic work.
- Take into consideration the natural order hypothesis: students need to be shown conventional uses of language when they are ready for them.

Sometimes in language workshop you might be focused on having students meet in groups, discuss their ideas about the theme of a text, and then share their ideas with the class. Perhaps they are focused on identifying character thoughts and feelings or the author's intention. When this is the focus of your workshop, then the lesson is a spontaneous language lesson (think process). However, if you want to teach new vocabulary or a new language structure so that the students can use it skillfully and understand it, then you will be teaching a scaffolded language lesson (think structure). Both process and structure lessons are part of a workshop focused on acquisition. Let's consider the difference by examining two lessons in language workshop.

Example of a Spontaneous Language Lesson
During the fall of 2004, I had the pleasure of working for two days with the teachers at Mary O. Pottenger School in Springfield, Massachusetts. There are many students of diverse backgrounds at the school, including many

English learners, mostly of Puerto Rican descent. One classroom I worked in was Araceli Santos' fifth-grade classroom, composed of many English learners and several language-minority students who were not English learners. I presented a lesson focused on getting the students to talk in a group about their ideas. They also needed to talk with partners and small groups had to share their ideas with the whole group. This was the first time these students had worked on language building in a workshop setting.

I focused the lesson on Allen Say's book *The Sign Painter* (2000). At first, the students were quiet and reluctant to speak up, but by the end of our time together, the students had created a list of questions regarding the text. I read parts of *The Sign Painter* and then paused to ask them what questions they had about the text. I recorded their questions on chart paper and referred back to the chart often as the discussion grew in intensity and length. It is typical for students new to language workshop to not speak up. Most of them didn't say much at first, but by the end of the lesson, almost all the students had contributed to the discussion and were talking with their partners about the topic (no easy feat with fifth-grade English learners!).

Two key factors helped this lesson go smoothly. One was that their teacher had a large meeting area on the floor (yes, even the fifth graders gathered on the floor). The second was that I made the conversation visual by writing down the ideas the students generated as we went. If an idea was new, or hit on the thinking I was pushing them toward (analysis), or included vocabulary that I thought might have been unfamiliar to some of the students, I color-coded the entry on the chart by circling it with a different-color marker. This lesson was a *process* lesson because it focused on getting the students to talk aloud with the large group, and with each other in pairs, about questions they had about the text and their ideas that answered some of the questions they had posed.

An Example of a Scaffolded Expression Lesson

Patti Politi teaches in a pullout ESL classroom for students new to English at Mary O. Pottenger School. In Patti's room I worked with one group of students who had acquired some English but were still in need of support both in conversational and academic language. Patti had been working on a unit of study focusing on family and immigration. She had read *Molly's Pilgrim* (Cohen 1998) to her students aloud. With Patti's help, the children had analyzed the events in the book and considered how the main character, Molly, was affected by those events. I worked with Patti's group to help them deepen their thinking and learn vocabulary for emotions.

I was impressed with the learning the students had completed in Patti's small classroom, but we were interested in pushing the children to think more about their learning, and Patti wanted the children to increase their abilities in English. Before I explain the *structure* lesson we focused on, it is important for you to know what Patti's teaching area looked like. Although Patti taught in a pullout setting, she had created an engaging classroom filled with print and books. She had created the culture of her room by arranging the furniture carefully. She had two easels, one with a pocket chart and one with chart paper, strategically arranged in front of a class meeting area. The pocket chart was filled with ideas and engaging vocabulary from recent literature books, and Patti routinely used the chart paper to make her lessons visual. The floor was covered with an engaging, whimsical carpet, and behind this meeting area were two tables (as opposed to desks) where children could meet in groups and sit side by side with their teacher. Around the perimeter of the teaching area were baskets of books, student work, and interesting reading materials full of language. The two walls near the meeting area were dripping with print and color. Patti's teaching area was engaging and *focused* on language. Patti had clearly considered the content, culture, and context of her room (see Chapter 2 for more on these classroom traits).

During this structure lesson, we focused on helping the children learn vocabulary for the emotions felt by the characters. I began the lesson by telling the students that events in books help us learn how characters feel. I gave an example from *Molly's Pilgrim*, and then told the children that we were going to consider the events in the book and think about how the characters felt. I made a triple T-chart on the chart paper and began by listing the first character we encountered while I read the book aloud. The chart looked like the example titled, Character Emotion Chart, in Appendix A. While I read, the children talked about what was happening in the book and how these things must have made the characters feel. The students sat in two groups and talked about how these events made them feel and then told me what to write on the chart. Without prompting from me, Patti's students identified emotion words like *sad* and *happy*. I wrote these on the chart and then added other words next to them, including *sorrow, happiness,* and *desperation*. After we read the book, the students talked in small groups about what happened at the end of the story and how the characters felt. Several of the students shared with the whole group about their ideas and used the new words I had listed instead of words like *sad*. Not only did they talk about the characters, but words bubbled up in conversation about how they felt sometimes with friends. Patti's students felt safe to take risks and try some of the new vocabulary while focused on discussing a book. They weren't told by Patti or me to use the new vocabulary, but by putting it on the chart, and talking about how the words were new ways to say what they already knew, we encouraged the children to use the new terminology.

Why Language Workshop Is Different

Language workshop focuses specifically on teaching children through content and cognitive processes. The two types of lessons in language workshop are process lessons and structure lessons. These lessons help us focus on providing instruction that encourages the acquisition of new language and opportunities to practice English in supportive and nurturing environments. The lessons also help us separate instruction on structure. It isn't appropriate to focus on structure all of the time, but when we do, we need to ensure that the lesson is driven by content and supported with scaffolded teaching through visuals and the authentic use of language. By teaching language in a workshop, we provide English learners and linguistically diverse students with the same high-quality, rigorous literacy program as their peers, but it is infused with language acquisition and the focus is on adding, not replacing language. Language workshop can help us

- Teach reading, writing, and language in a workshop based on a theory of balanced literacy instruction
- Develop student motivation through investigations into relevant topics in nonfiction and through strategic comprehension strategies in fiction
- Develop student engagement by involving students in both the process and the outcomes of learning
- Teach children to think and express themselves well through authentic experiences
- Infuse classrooms with rigor and quality
- Assess student knowledge, ability, and products in order to help children achieve more and acquire academic and social language
- Use real authors and student authors as mentors to improve writing, thinking, and reading comprehension
- Use standards and rubrics to show children how to think about their work and know how to improve
- Use writing as a way of knowing, learning, and understanding genres across the curriculum

CHAPTER FOUR

___

Understanding Language Acquisition

Early in October, Lori Garcia-Higgs, a first-grade teacher at my school, came into my office looking very worried. She asked, "Do you have a minute?"

"Yeah, what's up?"

"Well, I am worried about a few students in my room, and I just don't know what to do. I feel like I have tried all the things I know to do, and they are not making the growth I want for them. I need some advice."

"OK. Who are you worried about?" I asked as I pulled up a chair next to Lori.

"First, Sammy. He is an English learner and he isn't making much progress in reading. And then, Jose; he is also an English learner. He talks with me, but not out loud during group time on the carpet or during reading groups. I am *really* worried about him because he is repeating first grade. He still reads at a DRA level 3 [Beaver 2004]. And then, well, Kenisha." Lori paused.

"Tell me about Kenisha," I prodded.

"I'm worried about her, too. She isn't an English learner, but I don't think she has much language. She can read words, but she doesn't know what they mean. When I read aloud she doesn't talk or add to the discussion. I have more students who are quiet, but I'm really worried about her." Lori sat back in the chair and looked straight at me. "What can we do? I need help with these children."

I knew that Lori's question went deeper than a simple *What can we do?* She didn't need help with understanding the surface issues, like how students comprehend, or need to be given a cure-all task, like writing vocabulary cards; she needed to understand the deeper systemic issues of why these children were not learning like the other students in her class. I knew Lori came to me because the children were getting lost, in her classroom, in the school, and she wanted to stop this progression. Lori is a teacher who seeks information and answers to help children, and she had the children in her heart.

"Let's observe them together," I offered. I looked up at the clock. "Recess is almost over; I will be in right after the bell rings."

A few minutes later I settled into Lori's classroom with a legal pad and sharpened pencil in hand. The quick educational summary Lori gave me at recess reminded me of the student files I had been reading right before she had come to see me. While Lori was worried about her young learners, I was worried about many older learners in fifth and sixth grade who also were struggling in language and literacy. Some of the older learners were new to the school, and to the country, but many had been in our school since kindergarten.

I saw Kenisha from across the room and moved to sit near her. She was busy with her book box and was reading aloud to an imaginary friend, turning the book around every so often to show it to her "audience." She was reading leveled texts at Fountas and Pinnell (2005) levels D and E, but I noted from my discussion with Lori that Kenisha could read higher-level books but couldn't retell key ideas or explain the meaning of key words in the text. She wasn't an English learner like Sammy and Jose, but she needed a lot of language development.

Kenisha was working diligently at reading to her imaginary partner, twirling a tendril of her braided hair around her finger. "I would love it if you read to me, Kenisha," I said.

"OK!" she replied. Her eyes lit up and she began reading to me from one of her favorites.

For a moment, think of the children in your classroom. Do you have students like Sammy, Kenisha, or Jose? I worry about students in other teachers' classrooms all day long, because I want each one of them to be successful. However, worry alone is not enough. First, you need to watch the child, take notes, and truly understand what issues are affecting the child's learning (Owocki and Goodman 2002). Does the child need help with any of the following?

- Language development in order to acquire English (conversational and academic language)
- Language development as a native English speaker
- Reading comprehension strategy development
- Fluency development
- Practice in talking with peers and teachers about reading, ideas, and books

Understand Language Acquisition and Help Students Grow in Their Language Abilities

Children adding English are *acquiring* and not *learning* language (Freeman and Freeman 2003; Krashen 2003). Language acquisition is a subconscious

FIGURE 4.1   First Language Acquisition Factors

First Language Acquisition

- Parents model language in a safe and nurturing environment.
- While developing language, children have countless opportunities to try out language, interact with speakers, and receive modeling.
- Most children develop high levels of first language proficiency.
- First language acquisition is more internally motivated than second language acquisition, because an innate cognitive process is involved in learning a first language.

---

process; the learner acquires language without realizing it. When we acquire language, we use it to think, wonder, play, and talk (Rigg and Allen 1989). Children acquire a second language in some of the same ways that they learned their first language; however, there are subtle and important differences (Krashen 2003; Miramontes, Nadeau, and Commins 1997). Herrera and Murray (2005, 63) point out many differences between first and second language acquisition; a few of these factors, which affect children's learning in the classroom, are listed in Figures 4.1 and 4.2.

■ The children in Lori's class who speak English as their first language are in need of language development to continue acquiring more sophisticated levels of language.

FIGURE 4.2   Second Language Acquisition Factors

Second Language Acquisition

- Learners already have a language for communication and thinking.
- Peers and teachers are models for language.
- Learners can transfer thought processes from one language to the other.
- Learners can code switch, using key phrases in one or the other language to communicate greater meaning than if they relied only on one language.
- Second language acquisition is externally affected by sociocultural factors, and more externally motivated than first language acquisition (e.g., the learner chooses to learn the second language in order to do well in school, communicate, or get a job).
- Many learners do not acquire a high level of second language proficiency.
- Learners often have fewer opportunities to interact with second language models.
- Learners can lose a second language if they don't use it.

- The children in Lori's class who are acquiring English as a second language also need language development to increase their proficiency levels.

It is important to understand the needs of first and second language learners. Both are acquiring higher levels of English, but in different contexts and in different ways. Within the group of English learners in Lori's class, there were many children with varying abilities in English. In other words, they were at different stages in their process of acquiring English. While I was observing Kenisha and Jose, there was a group of students working with the bilingual aide, and there was one student new to the United States from Thailand working with Lori at her reading table. Kue sat very quietly while Lori showed him common objects in classrooms in the United States and told him the names of each object. Kenisha was acquiring higher levels of English as a monolingual speaker, while Jose and Sammy were acquiring English as English learners.

Stages of Language Acquisition

Learners acquire language in five stages described in Krashen's natural order hypothesis (Cummins 1991; Freeman and Freeman 1998; Krashen 2003; Herrera and Murray 2005). This hypothesis implies that there is a general, predictable order to the process in which a student of any age acquires a second language. Krashen (2003, 2) states, "Not every acquirer proceeds in exactly the same order, but the variation among acquirers is not extreme. There is clearly an 'average' order of acquisition." Krashen goes on to state *three amazing facts* about the natural order of learning language:

- First, the order is not based on any language features of simplicity or complexity. So the order you may perceive to be easy to learn, and therefore to teach, is not necessarily how the brain will acquire language.
- Second, the natural order cannot be changed. Purposeful teaching of grammar skills will not make a student acquire a language function faster than the student would normally acquire it.
- Third, the natural order is not a teaching order because learners acquire language through comprehensible messages, communication, and information. Also, students acquire language at different rates and in their own way, so when children are exposed to rich, comprehensible contexts, they will acquire language in a natural order as they are ready. (Krashen 2003, 2)

These facts are important to remember when thinking of the *English learners* in your classroom:

- Students acquire a second language in a natural order.
- Students acquire parts of language *when they are ready*; this order cannot be affected by specific teaching of grammar skills.

- Students need exposure to interesting and comprehensible information, messages, and language models; then they will absorb the language and develop competency.

There are also important facts to remember for children *speaking English as their first language*:

- Children need exposure to high-interest, informative language models to increase their levels of language.
- Children acquire their first language in an innate manner from nurturing, accepting models who provide rich language experiences.
- Children need innumerable experiences with language. (Peregoy and Boyle 1997)

The natural order hypothesis suggests five stages of language acquisition that are generally accepted and used to level English learners through assessment. These stages are:

preproduction

early production

speech emergence

intermediate fluency

advanced fluency

You may receive test scores from your administrator labeling each student who is learning English with a level that generally applies to one of these five stages. While language acquisition moves from stage to stage, I strongly encourage you to keep in mind Krashen's amazing three facts about language acquisition and loosely apply the stages to your students' abilities, as social and academic situations can cause a child to be less confident and less fluent in English than other, more comfortable and familiar situations. What is important is what language abilities the children have in your classroom, and can apply to learning, not what a test score says about their ability.

Political Contexts of Language Teaching

We are at a time in education where English language acquisition and English language arts achievement are expected to occur simultaneously. This educational context is also a political context; politicians and voters have established much current policy in the education of English learners (Garcia 2003). In addition, standardized test results are used to publicly grade schools; there is great public pressure for schools to obtain high test scores. English learners, and students of poverty in need of outstanding literacy instruction, can get lost in the shuffle of test-driven curricula (McNeil 2000). Current policy in California expects teachers to move children quickly to "proficiency" in English, through English only without the aid of first language support or instruction. I cannot imagine how difficult this is for children.

As a speaker of two other languages, I remember how it felt to attempt to communicate informally at work while learning to speak Spanish and at home while learning to speak Farsi. Today, I am constantly reminded of my limitations in both languages when I am trying to explain something to a parent, or a child, and I don't have the right words, or when I get lost in the language at home because I don't have a very well developed vocabulary in Farsi. And my experiences are all social situations. I cannot imagine being plunged all day long into learning in a language I don't understand and then being expected to achieve high levels of literacy at the same time.

Because of the context of language learning, immersion programs, not primary bilingual programs, seem to be the norm (Garcia 2003). Considering the context, and the rich research background in language acquisition, as teachers we must work for the implementation of effective programs that develop language in natural and stimulating ways and encourage students to be empowered by knowledge and school. Standardized or basal programs do not provide all the parts of an effective program for English learners and current educational policy ignores the bulk of educational research and experience in language acquisition over the last twenty years (Short and Echevarría 2004; Garcia, 2003). English learners need instruction targeted to their developmental needs and differentiated for language development (Helman 2005). Therefore, teachers must become the professionals who ensure that English learners reach the highest levels of academic and personal success.

English learners in our schools need teachers who understand effective pedagogy, cultural situations, and the emotions of children learning English and children who are immigrants. As teachers we must envision things for these children that they cannot envision for themselves. When facing programs or issues that don't make sense for our classrooms, one option that seems to be effective for English learners is to immerse them in classrooms where they are exposed to wonderful, rich language in a variety of forms and functions and given authentic opportunities to use language in reading, writing, listening, and speaking. If children are immersed in English, they need plenty of opportunities to use their first language to help them build understanding and communicate. Teachers must be very thoughtful in developing lessons so that language, literacy, and content knowledge do not suffer while the students acquire English.

The optimal program for supporting English learners and providing opportunities for academic success is primary language instruction (Thomas and Collier 1997a; Ramirez, Yuen, and Ramey 1991). There are many versions of bilingual programs including early-exit, late-exit, and two-way programs (Thomas and Collier 1997b). Whatever program children are learning in, students in bilingual programs have the opportunity to develop English, to develop cognitively challenging content knowledge, and to continue developing their first language, which in turns aids student learning, adjustment, and success in school (Herrera and Murray 2005). A discussion of bilingual education is beyond the scope of this book; however, instruction in students' primary language affords children and adolescents an education, time to acquire English, and the opportunity to become bilingual and biliterate, thus contributing to our diverse global community.

When working with students in English, it is important that the language is comprehensible. Comprehensible input is information that is understandable to the learner (Peregoy and Boyle 1997). We are able to acquire language in a natural way when we understand messages in an authentic context (Krashen 2003).

Know Your Students: Assessment of Acquisition

Changing your instruction to help children learn means changing practice to increase equity and access for English learners. On the other hand, using assessment information to label children and unknowingly limit their potential will not help them achieve in school or acquire English. I am guilty of labeling a student myself, and it limited my vision for what the child could achieve that year. Several years ago, when I taught third grade, Maria joined my class in October. Maria had moved around the state several times; she had emigrated from Mexico two years prior. Maria was an outgoing and exceptionally open and friendly child. She talked with everyone. She talked with me, with her friends in the lunch line, with classmates at recess. She talked with the principal, with the secretary, and with the cafeteria servers. She talked in class during share time, during story time, and even during the times when I didn't want her to talk!

Because of her oral fluency in English, I assumed (falsely) that Maria had acquired an equally verbose language bank in academic subjects. I first noticed a problem in reading group. Maria would read well orally, and she would read lots of small chapter books on her own (she had been schooled in Spanish in Mexico and began reading in English in third grade), but she wasn't comprehending what she was reading. She couldn't tell me who the characters in her book were or what they were doing. Her lack of academic language was more noticeable during social studies. She did not participate in class discussions and would be unusually quiet. Finally, one day it hit me: I was so confident in her level of acquisition because of her oral ability in conversation. I didn't consider that she had not acquired academic language and was in need of language development—content-based English language development and sheltered content area instruction. I was upset and embarrassed about my oversight.

This "aha" that struck me is all too common in classrooms. Children appear to be fluent orally and in casual conversation because they have developed *conversational fluency*. Conversational fluency refers to the language that most children posses in their native language when beginning kindergarten (Cummins 2003). Most English learners develop conversational fluency in two to three years of acquiring English (Cummins 2003;

Thomas and Collier 1997a, 1997b). What Maria lacked was *academic language proficiency*. This language dimension includes domain, or content-specific, vocabulary in English and the ability to produce and understand complex written and oral language (Cummins 1989, 2003). This is the language proficiency evident when an English learner takes tests, participates in a literature circle, and reads nonfiction or complex fiction. The development of academic language is often taken for granted by nonlanguage teachers and once children are orally fluent in conversation, sometimes they are viewed as proficient in English, which is not true.

Another dimension of language proficiency is discrete language skills, or the development of specific phonological, grammatical, reading, and writing knowledge that students acquire as a result of direct instruction and practice (Cummins 2003; Herrera and Murray 2005). These are skills that a child may learn in a minilesson during reading instruction or in a whole-group writing lesson. However, it is important to remember that this dimension of language proficiency is focused on language learning. The student has to remember the rule or point taught. It is a less natural sequence, but when a student is ready, this type of learning can help him apply skills for public speaking or polished writing, or gain confidence in preparing work for presentation.

The three dimensions of language proficiency are

- Conversational fluency—the ability to carry on face-to-face conversation
- Discrete language skills—specific phonological, literacy, and grammatical knowledge that students acquire
- Academic language proficiency—knowledge of less frequent vocabulary and the ability to interpret and produce increasingly complex language

These dimensions are not entirely separate from one another; they develop concurrently. However, understanding what each dimension consists of is important for understanding student abilities and needs. Different instructional experiences promote different dimensions.

What saved both Maria and me was switching my focus from assuming what she knew to assessing her abilities in order to find her strengths and then plan instruction. I had to consider her conversational skills, academic language, and discrete language knowledge. Wong Fillmore (1999) suggests that truly assessing and understanding the needs of the English learner means considering the student's schooling experiences in light of five environmental components that affect language learning:

- Motivating students to learn English and recognize the importance of learning the language well
- Providing excellent language models for English learners that illustrate underlying form, structure, and meaning (the learner should have access to good language models as she transitions to more sophisticated levels of English acquisition)

- Providing an interactive learning setting (there needs to be enough student-teacher interaction, individually and in small groups, so that learning can take place)
- Giving feedback and social support in order to help English learners extend beyond their current level of knowledge
- Practicing English many, many times throughout the day in various group settings

When considering Maria, I took anecdotal notes on her reading and her writing abilities; I considered favorite subjects and what subjects she showed more confidence in academically. I also considered the social components suggested by Wong Fillmore and wrote reflective notes on the classroom environment and instruction I was providing. I analyzed my notes and planned instruction for Maria. My instruction was based on an additive philosophy: I had to consider what Maria already knew (she could talk to anyone without hesitation!) and then add to her knowledge. In order to build academic language and appropriate discrete language knowledge, I planned lessons rich in content and information while providing support so that Maria could participate and learn. I did not focus on reducing my lessons to small bits and pieces so that Maria could learn little snippets one at a time, which is a reductionist view of instruction (Cummins 2003). Instead, I assumed that with proper scaffolding and language support to make the academic language comprehensible, Maria would acquire the next language structures for which her brain was ready. I worked to create a language workshop in my classroom.

Focusing on Students

One of the most difficult tasks we face as teachers is to communicate across our individual differences (Delpit 1989). As language teachers it is important to understand how students acquire language, how they view school, and how they feel about their schooling experiences. It is our duty to bridge the language and social gaps that exist. Our overly positive or negative perceptions of our students can harm them. Sometimes I hear a teacher lament a child's lack of language. But think about that statement. All children have language; it is a matter of identifying what language a child uses to communicate at home and understanding how the child uses language. Perhaps what is occurring in the child's life doesn't match our preconceived notion of how things are supposed to be. Most likely the child can communicate at home, but doesn't know how to communicate at school or isn't comfortable doing so. Our perception of children's abilities is based on assumptions that we reinforce in typical classroom activities and exchanges. This is also true for students who are poor readers. Students who fall behind in the development of early literacy skills have fewer opportunities to practice reading and participate in literate discourses; often they never catch up with mainstream peers.

We have to be careful. Listen to the child and note his strengths to avoid limiting his potential. By carefully assessing and gathering information about the child's use of language beyond our classroom doors, we can avoid implementing a self-fulfilling prophecy. Often children live up to the expectations we set for them (Winograd, Flores-Dueñas, and Arrington 2003). Our values lead to our perspectives, which lead to our actions. Be reflective, be conscious of your instruction, and increase opportunities for student success. The children need passionate teachers who understand their backgrounds and needs as immigrants and language learners.

CHAPTER FIVE

The Wonder of Words
Promoting Vocabulary Development

Vocabulary development! There, I said it. Wow, it feels good to get it out there. Perhaps this whole time you've been wondering when I was going to discuss vocabulary development. Recently, vocabulary has become a key focus in our classrooms; current literature in education points to an underdeveloped vocabulary to explain why students don't read well, why English learners don't have academic language, and why more students don't score higher on standardized tests. *It's vocabulary*. So, how do we tackle enriching our students' vocabularies while maintaining an effective classroom and a balanced literacy program?

First, we don't have enough time in the day, week, month, or year to teach all the words a student can possibly need to know. On average, students add two thousand to three thousand words to their repertoires each year (Beck, McKeown, and Kucan 2002; Lehr, Osborn, and Hiebert 2004). Second, every time I see a teacher who thinks that vocabulary development means teaching *words*, I see lists of words on the board and, at some point during the day, kids looking up definitions in dictionaries. But this isn't best practice in any classroom, especially a classroom filled with English learners and linguistic-minority children. Vocabulary instruction is about more than words. It is about the conceptual understanding of what words mean.

Words guide us, drench us in meaning, power, utility, and intelligence. Knowledge of them can unlock doors and bring pleasure because beautiful words are fulfilling to know, understand, and say. Words connected to content studies give us knowledge of ideas and the world.

It's true. Think of words that you find fabulous to roll off your tongue; here are a few of my favorites: *vacillate, effervescent, capitulate, hullabaloo, opulent*. Words that you find wondrous might make you think deeply about what you are reading or make you feel on top of your game. Sometimes I read something so beautiful, so simple, and so well said that for a moment I forget to breathe. It is the power of the words chosen by the author to convey a message that connects in an intensely personal way to my life. The same is true for our students. Words unlock the future for children who have vocabularies large enough to develop their knowledge base. Words can

- aid comprehension as children read
- help them sound honest and smart when writing
- help them speak well

There is nothing I find more pleasurable than having a book talk with a group of students who are able to discuss the book, state their thoughts, and use powerful vocabulary during the conversation. I feel the same way when I read children's writing and see beautiful words woven into their work. I am awed not because the children were prompted to use the vocabulary words, but because the words are part of who they are, and they are becoming literate. Words hold power.

The situation is urgent for English learners and linguistic-minority children. A large gap exists between mainstream children, who come to school knowing many words, and minority students, particularly Latino children, in national assessments (Carlo et al. 2004). Because reading development is directly tied to the breadth and depth of a student's vocabulary, a lack of a well-developed vocabulary makes it hard for linguistic-minority students to catch up. While the situation isn't dire in the primary grades, as children move to upper grades, where they have fewer opportunities to learn to read and are expected to read to learn, achievement plunges (Biemiller 1999; Chall and Jacobs 1996). Their vocabularies are too limited to maintain fluency and comprehension in the rich, demanding texts found in middle and high school. These students don't have a repertoire of words in domain knowledge to aid their content comprehension. Domain knowledge includes knowledge of specific words and concepts associated with content areas (Liben and Liben 2005).

Powerful Vocabulary Instruction

If we want to ensure that English learners and language-minority students have access to the wonder of words, and the power that a well-developed vocabulary affords, then we have to teach vocabulary development explicitly. *How* we teach is the key issue.

Teaching vocabulary well focuses on

- Knowing concepts that words represent
- Demonstrating that a large repertoire of words readily available in your mind and classroom helps you read, think, speak, and write
- Teaching ideas, not words
- Choosing words selectively and not teaching endless lists of words
- Discussing words, focusing on related words, and creating semantic representations of words
- Actively engaging students with authentic vocabulary work

Chapter Five

This call for vocabulary instruction can be implemented in classrooms in a variety of ways; I want to focus on what is most effective for English learners and language-minority students. As reviewed earlier, the classroom serving language-minority children needs a teacher's guidance and perseverance to close the achievement gap. The teacher needs to understand how to implement connected, thematic, and coherent instruction. This is true for vocabulary instruction as well. Teaching bits and pieces of vocabulary lists isn't going to help very much because our brains seek patterns, relevance, and connections. (See Figure 5.1.) That is why the best instruction connects words to other ideas and language knowledge. We have to see where word *development* fits into our day.

This is a big idea to grasp, so think of an effective framework for vocabulary development as three intersecting circles. Each circle is important, and without it, an essential piece of the program would be missing. One circle is vocabulary development through free reading, another circle is vocabulary development through precise and rich word *concept* instruction, and the third circle is vocabulary development tied to units of study. (See Part 3 of the book for in-depth unit-of-study lesson plans and ideas.) A child-centered classroom focuses on best practices that foster learning. Without one part, the classroom workshop would be less rich and less effective. When the three parts of vocabulary instruction are in place, the teacher strives to use language that enriches the atmosphere, piques student interest and imagination, and raises the bar on expectation in the room (Beck, McKeown, and Kucan 2002; Carlo et al. 2004; Herrell and Jordan 2004). Instruction is

- rich
- full of new contexts and new words to describe the contexts

FIGURE 5.1 Heart of Vocabulary Instruction

Our brains seek patterns, relevance, and connection.
This is the heart of vocabulary instruction. The best vocabulary instruction goes beyond teaching definitions and context. It focuses on

- word concepts
- the wonder of words—what appeals to students and why
- connections among words
- ways in which words link thoughts and concepts
- incidental word acquisition through reading
- powerful instruction that doesn't teach labels and definitions

Remember: Great vocabulary instruction focuses on developing an understanding of the interconnectivity between words, concepts, and word use in literature and literary nonfiction.

- focused on students becoming literate
  - the teacher models vocabulary in everyday conversation
  - the teacher shows his passion for certain words and explains why
- fascinating
- connected to thematic units

Extensive Reading Promotes Vocabulary Acquisition

Vocabulary instruction occurs in more than one way. First, students acquire incidental vocabulary words through reading. They need to read texts at their level—books of interest, magazines, and any other material that gets them motivated. They need to read every day for a minimum of thirty minutes to develop their vocabularies. They must read, and read a lot. So the first way you can directly improve your students' vocabularies is by setting up a time in your daily schedule for reading just right books. Remember, a just right book is one in which the student knows and can read correctly 97 percent of the words. That means that the student miscues only *three* times out of one hundred words (Fountas and Pinnell 1996). It seems obvious that reading broadly (various genres and materials) and widely (several works by one author or on one topic) should be occurring in our classrooms. But this is not necessarily the case. Often students are not reading enough in our programs or in conjunction with our programs.

Free reading is the best prediction of vocabulary growth between second and fifth grade (Cunningham and Stanovich 1998; Anderson, Wilson, and Fielding 1998). Students acquire a large amount of words per year during free reading (Nagy 1988; Krashen 2003). This is one reason it is so important to support, scaffold, and insist on free reading in class *and* out of class. You cannot assume that because you suggest it, a student will read; you have to create the context for this to occur. Even though students will learn a lot of vocabulary through reading, there are many words that they need to experience and use repeatedly until the words become part of their repertoires. Nagy and Anderson (1984) researched word groups and families. They found that school texts from grades 3 to 9 have approximately 88,500 distinct word families. That is a lot of words!

While reading certainly helps vocabulary development, students need additional support, especially English learners at the intermediate stages of language acquisition (Carlo et al. 2004). These are the students who *seem* fluent during conversation but still struggle to comprehend content area texts. Thinking of teaching 88,500 word families is overwhelming and it's really not necessary. Beck, McKeown, and Kucan (2002) suggest teaching about 400 words each year, keeping in mind that a bulk of the words will be learned incidentally through reading, discussion, and read-alouds. I recommend focusing on 8 to 10 words each week (Lehr, Osborn, and Hiebert 2004). If you are teaching these words within rich and interconnected discussions, other words will come up naturally, but the magic 8 to 10 words can guide your instruction without overwhelming your students with unconnected learning. It is important to be selective in order to be effective in teaching vocabulary.

In addition to ensuring free reading, you need to develop explanations of familiar concepts during reading and help students relate this knowledge to new words they are learning (Shefelbine 2004). This means giving children new names for something they already know. If they understand that Maria Isabel in *My Name Is Maria Isabel* (Ada 1995) felt sad when rejected by other students and this bothered her for a long time, students can learn words connected to those concepts, like *depressed* and *rejected*. You need to provide descriptive explanations: Shefelbine (2004) calls these *parenthetical explanations* (use the word *parenthesis* to help you remember the meaning of *parenthetical*). A parenthetical explanation is one with lots of additional information (in other words, the teacher talks about the word, gives examples of the word in context, and the students add their thinking to the conversation) that builds understanding. That is, an explanation just like one in the previous sentence; I added extra ideas to develop the concept of parenthetical explanations.

Teach Concepts, *Not Words*

Don't teach words! Teach concepts. This idea may be new to you, but it is a proven method and has been recommended for many years (Biemiller 1999; Beck, McKeown, and Kucan 2002; Nagy 1988). Looking up words in the dictionary is not pedagogically sound; however, I see this practiced in classrooms more often than rich, direct vocabulary lessons. Vocabulary development isn't about a student learning lists of words that are identified for a grade level. It is about teaching concepts about words so that children can make sense of new information and categorize this information into learning. Remember that the brain is continually seeking patterns and relevance (Wolfe 2001). So when we teach isolated lists of words, we are working against the natural function of the brain. As language teachers, we need to focus on helping the brain make sense of new information and connect with and retain (or acquire) the new information. This way we develop minds as well as teach.

To focus on teaching word concepts, combine definition and contextual approaches related to what the concept of the word is. For example, if I were to introduce the word *brief* to students, I would discuss *brief* and give multiple examples of what *brief* could mean and how it could be used. I might say:

- I like when some things are *brief*, like a wait at a stoplight.
- I don't like when other things are *brief* like recess. Who likes a short recess? Well, I don't either. When recess is *brief*, I don't have enough time to get ready for our next lesson.
- Sonia, why don't you like *brief* recesses?
- Is there anything else you like or don't like that is *brief*?

When students share their ideas about a word, we are discussing the concept of the word. (I am connecting the parenthetical explanation to known ideas for students and therefore helping their brains connect patterns together.) I can continue the lesson by writing the word on a sentence strip and adding it our "Wondrous Words" board or to our "Powerful Words" board. I can also add words related to *brief* in concept: *abridged, concise, scanty, short,* and *reduced*. I can also add the antonyms to the board on opposites: *extended, lengthy, long,* and *protracted* (Houghton Mifflin 1998).

If I teach vocabulary this way in my language workshop, I have to ensure that I am focusing on

- adequate definitions
- illustrations of word meanings in natural-sounding contexts
- connecting the words back to the conversation
- modeling the word use orally and in writing
- putting the words up on the walls as resources that students can return to over and over

Content-Specific Word Learning in the Language Workshop

The third circle (see page 37) is teaching vocabulary through the units of study that guide the language workshop over the course of a year. The units of study fold out over three to four weeks and are grounded in expectations for genre, content, or strategy work. Vocabulary development should mirror the current unit; teachers should explain concepts using correct vocabulary and then expect students to use it.

For example, Figures 5.2 and 5.3 are pieces of student work from a lesson I taught in Mary O. Pottenger School in November 2004. This lesson is from a language workshop demonstration in second grade where I focused students on character actions and traits. I had explained to students we were going to discuss character actions and traits (two vocabulary concepts) and then talk about the traits of Molly in the book *Molly Lou Melon* (Lovell 2001). Elimarie wrote about Molly's traits using key vocabulary that came from my lesson (see Figure 5.2). The two words that triggered Elimarie's understanding of word concepts were *brave* and *lesson*. Specifically, Elimarie explained what *brave* meant to her: "I think that Molly is braver than anybody. Because she is brave to talk back." And she explained the term *new lesson* by showing that Ronald learned a new lesson because Molly's friends think she is better than everybody else. A second example is Janelis' piece in Figure 5.3, Janelis wrote about Molly Lou's bravery by describing how the character was "not scared that she was little." Janelis also synthesized information by discussing how Molly Lou taught Ronald how to be good. Both girls wrote their ideas about the character traits and actions and synthesized the information by choosing a theme for Molly's actions.

Three Keys to Powerful Conceptual Teaching

There are three main ideas to remember when implementing vocabulary instruction. These are the keys that in combination will provide your stu-

FIGURE 5.2   Elimarie's Piece

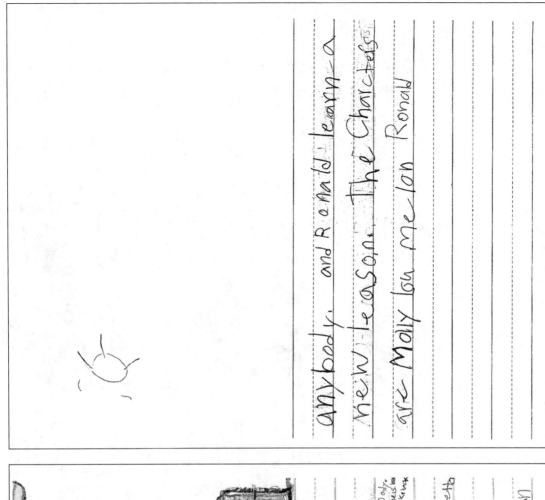

FIGURE 5.3 Janelis' Piece

dents with powerful instruction connected to ideas that will help them acquire the words:

- integration
- repetition
- meaningful use (Nagy 1988)

These three keys are important because students usually learn words gradually, and the more vocabulary is integrated into current instruction, connected to prior knowledge, repeated, and used in meaningful ways, the more likely students are to learn the words (Lehr, Osborn, and Hiebert 2004; Richek 2005).

Integration

To integrate vocabulary instruction, connect words to a theme or unit of study. Integration activates background knowledge. When we integrate new words with known information, we help our students connect to the unknown words and content information. Integrating vocabulary instruction within content studies helps students develop domain knowledge, that is, information and vocabulary we accrue in different areas as we read and learn (Hirsch 2003). If we have domain knowledge about oceans, we can connect to and better understand a text on oceanography. It is important for our students to develop domain knowledge in a variety of areas, from the grade-level content studies to reading comprehension strategies. Domain knowledge helps with reading comprehension and helps us develop an understanding of our world. So when we integrate vocabulary instruction, we are not only expanding students' vocabularies but helping them develop knowledge that will aid their learning and reading comprehension.

Integration is an outgrowth of schema theory. Schema theory views knowledge as a network of mental structures that represent our understanding of the world (Davis 1991). So when we teach vocabulary connected to an idea, or schema, we already have, then the vocabulary is more easily retained. Schema theory also explains how our brains make sense of text as we read. The reader's knowledge (schema), expectations, and use of reading strategies determine the meaning the reader brings to the text (Anderson and Pearson 1984). Just as in vocabulary instruction, the reader adds new knowledge gained in reading into an existing schema, or adapts a schema to include the new information. Schema theory explains how English learners' experiences, background knowledge, and understanding of how the world works have a critical connection to their development of academic English (Scarcella 2003). If the students have limited background, or a limited understanding of words, ideas, and information, it becomes more critical to teach connected, coherent language in our classrooms.

When the teacher focuses on schema theory during instruction, he might

- Help students build schemata and make connections between ideas
- Build connections between ideas with word cards, story maps, semantic maps, illustrations, songs, poetry, and word plays

- Remind his students of what they already know before introducing new material
- Provide time for students to assimilate new ideas (and words) into existing schemata; learning is a process (Davis 1991)

There are many ways to design lessons that focus on integration, but all lessons should connect words to existing ideas, support students with visual aids, and stretch their brains to assimilate new information. Teaching approaches include semantic maps, semantic impressions, word expert cards, semantic feature analysis charts, Venn diagrams, linear arrays, and word journals (Beck, McKeown, and Kucan 2002; Lehr, Osborn, and Hiebert 2004; Nagy 1988; Richek 2005). See Figure 5.4 for an explanation of some of these strategies.

FIGURE 5.4   Vocabulary Lesson Strategies

Lesson	Explanation	Example
semantic maps	Can be used to teach vocabulary in preparation to read a book or article in a content area. A concept word goes in the middle box and related words, or phrases related to the theme or concept, are diagrammed around the main word.	
semantic impressions	Students take a list of words from a book and create their own story out of the words *before* reading the text. (from Richek 2005)	Words from *Names for Snow* (Beach 2003) *welcome, stretch, crook, lace, lilac, embroiders, stillness* Story example: In the morning, I *welcomed* the warm sun that shone on my face and on the *lilacs* in my garden. My cat lay in the *stillness* of the sunshine, but when I went into the garden she *stretched*, jumped into my arms, and settled into the *crook* of my elbow. The *lace* on my *embroidered* shirt tickled her whiskers as she slept.
word expert cards	Students create cards that include a visual representation of the word, the definition, the part of speech, a student-created sentence using the word, and the student's personal definition of the word. (from Richek 2005)	

FIGURE 5.4 *(Continued)*

Lesson	Explanation	Example				

Lesson	Explanation		Modern Travel	Used with Animals	For Children	Used for Air Travel
semantic feature analysis chart	Establishes connections between words. The array displays the relationships among word meanings. This works best for words closely related in meaning. The words are placed in a chart with a group of words running down the left column and the semantic features running across the top of the chart. Semantic features are concepts that describe components of meanings.	Buggy		X	X	
		Car	X		X	
		Rocket	X			X
		Wagon		X	X	
		Airplane	X		X	X
		Pram			X	
		Cart		X	X	

Lesson	Explanation	Example
Venn diagrams	Compare and contrast words that represent concepts or level two words from content or genre studies. Level two words appear frequently in reading and are part of a mature student's vocabulary. The common words in the intersecting point relate to the content or genre.	Weather Words Hot — Cold Blistering, Sweltering, Roasting, Steaming, Broiling Sun, Wind, Rain, Snow, Sleet, Fog, Air pressure Freezing, Subzero, Icy, Chilly, Glacial, Bitter
linear arrays	Show relationship between words by arranging in a line. Compare and contrast words to develop a refined understanding of nuances between word meanings. Sequences can be based on intensity, size, position, or order. (from Nagy 1988)	*annoyed, angry, enraged, furious* *warm, hot, blistering, torrid*
word journals	Student-kept journal listing favorite words, beautiful words, interesting words, and words student wants to remember.	Student records the word, the definition of the word, a picture representing the word, and the source where the student first heard or read the word.

Repetition and Meaningful Use

The other two keys of meaningful vocabulary instruction are repetition and meaningful use. In great classroom practice, these are rarely separated; children need time to learn, but they also need experiences that are meaningful and engaging. For instance, let's say that you are introducing a set of words your students need to know for a unit on travel in the 1700s. The class has been studying the American Revolution, and your students will be taking a field trip to a ship docked in a nearby port. Now, you could post a list of words and discuss them often, and even assign students to write sentences using the words. But if your goal is to provide rich and powerful vocabulary instruction in a connected classroom, then your instruction might look a bit different.

In this integrated unit on the American Revolution, the vocabulary is embedded in the content. Figure 5.5 shows an example of a semantic map of *ship* vocabulary from Susan Harper's classroom at Pinedale Elementary School. She created this map *with* the students. It is important to create the map with the students because the connections between ideas and words

FIGURE 5.5   Semantic Map on Ship Vocabulary

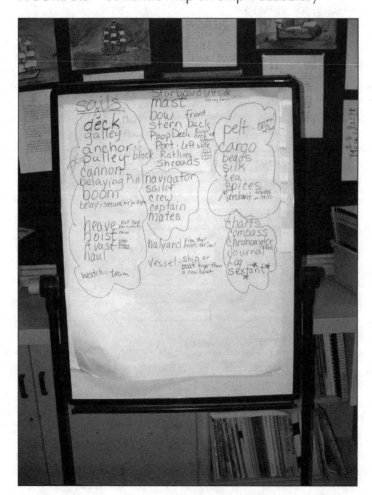

need to occur in their brains as you create the map, discuss the map, and modify the map (see Appendix A for a vocabulary web template, which is a type of semantic map). In Susan's example she listed the vocabulary in related word bubbles.

Figure 5.6 shows more examples of semantic maps. These charts are from Cary Stolpestad's classroom at Manchester GATE Elementary School in Fresno, California. You can see how Cary displayed several semantic maps all related to her theme of California history. Some of the base words in the middle of the maps are ideas that are tied to the background knowledge needed for her students to understand what they will be reading and learning. Beck, McKeown, and Kucan (2002) calls these tier two words (see next section for more on this). Other words on Cary's maps are tier three words, which are words directly connected to a specific unit of study.

Another great example of powerful vocabulary instruction comes from Laurie Cruz's classroom at Pinedale Elementary (see Figure 5.7). Laurie has her students represent words visually. She often gives them index cards and has them write a word on one side of the card and write a definition in their own words and draw a picture to represent the word on the reverse side. Figure 5.8 shows an example of a class chart with words broken into prefixes and suffixes and with pictures that represent the meanings of the words.

These activities are powerful because the teacher creates the charts with the students while facilitating a discussion regarding the new words that both students and the teacher suggest adding to the chart. It's important to ask students if a word applies, or doesn't apply, to the base word, or related

FIGURE 5.6 Cary's Vocabulary Charts

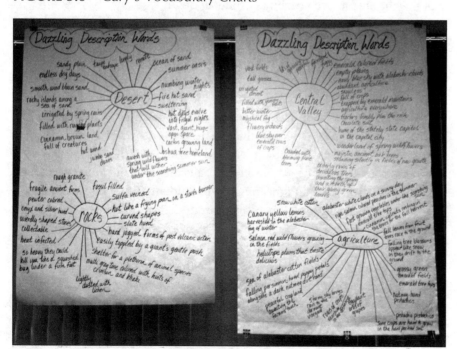

FIGURE 5.7 Picture Representations of Vocabulary Words

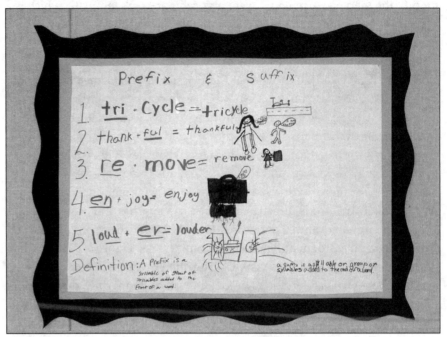

words, and if so, why (Nagy 1988). The students need to be actively engaged in creating the map, or vocabulary chart, so that they own it. They need to be part of the thinking in order to understand the chart when they review it for reference; then they'll feel that they are getting it (see Figure 5.8). It is really important for the students to feel like they *get it*; only then will they be able to use vocabulary independently.

For learning to occur, vocabulary instruction needs to be repeated. But this doesn't mean drill and kill. The repetition must be couched in meaningful use, the third key to vocabulary instruction (Nagy 1988; Richek 2005). When a student hears a word several times, and has opportunities to use the word, she will be most likely to learn the word. Repetition and meaningful use go hand in hand for powerful and purposeful vocabulary instruction. Stahl (2003) suggests that we need to encounter a word twelve times to learn it and be able to understand it while reading. Numerous encounters to learn and truly know a word calls for repetition, but this repetition must be connected and meaningful for students. Students have to practice new learning until it becomes part of their repertoires. Willingham (2004) calls this *practicing beyond the point of perfection*. Language-minority students need to understand how and why we use certain words and how to select appropriate words. This should be the goal of our practice time. Practicing for accurate production of words won't teach our students to think about word usage and try to truly understand what a word means.

Susan Harper gave her students opportunities for meaningful practice in her classroom in a variety of ways. She handed out pictures of the trip

FIGURE 5.8   Creating Vocabulary Charts

Creating Vocabulary Charts

Remember: Create the charts used in your room *with* your students.
Don't retype them after school and make them beautiful. The
connections the children made during this experience will be lost and
then the chart will become "wallpaper" in your room. For powerful
recognition and memory triggering, leave the chart as you created it
with students. Unless, of course, you add new words *with* your class.
Classroom vocabulary charts are

- created with students
- discussed with students
- revised with students

---

they took to the ship and then asked students to work with their partners to
discuss the memories triggered by the pictures. Students looked at the vocabulary map often and Susan encouraged them to use the correct words.
When I sat and listened to Jose and Kue share, I heard Jose say, "I bent
down and looked through the porthole." Then he glanced at the vocabulary
chart, nodded his head, and continued, "and then through the porthole,
Mrs. Harper took this picture of me."

How to Choose Words for Intensive Instruction

It is important to be selective in choosing words to teach. It is not possible
to teach all unknown words in a text. In fact, it isn't desirable to do so because students need to develop word-solving skills while reading, and
some words are so rare that fully developing student knowledge of them
isn't necessary (Armbuster, Lehr, and Osborn 2001; Shefelbine 2004). Remember the focus on vocabulary instruction is a short, powerful, precise
time to teach children to *love* words and learn new ones. To help you organize for instruction, focus on these ideas:

- Most texts have too many unknown words to teach all with direct
  instruction.
- Direct vocabulary instruction can take a lot of class time, and students
  will acquire many words while reading.
- Students should practice word-solving and word-learning strategies to
  independently learn word meanings.
- Words serve different linguistic purposes and have different levels of
  importance.
- A word's usefulness in a text points to the importance of the word for
  instruction.

Beck, McKeown, and Kucan (2002) suggest that good vocabulary instruction places major consideration on a word's usefulness and frequency of use. They organize words in three categories. Each category has a different level of word type and use. They place importance on teaching tier two words.

- Tier one: Basic words that rarely need instruction. For example: *house, mother, sing*.
- Tier two: Words that appear frequently in reading, are part of a mature reader's and writer's vocabulary, and are found across a variety of content areas and genres. These words tend to be conceptually difficult for an inexperienced reader or writer. For example: *responsibility, curious, captain*.
- Tier three: Words that are connected to a specific domain of knowledge and appear infrequently in text. These words are best learned while studying a content area. For example: *cirrus, isotope*.

Remember the two important points of tier two words:

- high frequency
- useful addition to students' vocabularies

Think of helping students identify and know words. If they are able to reflect upon the word you have selected for instruction, you can better focus your vocabulary instruction. Think of it as having students preassess their own knowledge and then follow up by reflecting on what they have learned. Students need to determine whether they have heard of a word, know it and can use it, or if they know it well enough to teach the word to someone else. Figure 5.9 is an example of a graphic organizer for reflective assessment.

Linking Vocabulary and Reading Instruction

While there is no single direct method to ensure that vocabulary instruction supports students' comprehension development, research has shown that effective instruction uses a variety of methods (Lehr, Osborn, and Hiebert 2004). The National Reading Panel analyzed the body of research on vocabulary instruction and reading development and found that vocabulary instruction does improve reading comprehension as long as the method is matched to the age and abilities of the child (NICHHD 2000). This is important to remember: the instruction we provide in an interconnected model of vocabulary development must be appropriate to the students we work with. This seems like a simple concept, but sometimes it is easy to water down curriculum for students learning English or students with less enriched backgrounds. They need appropriate instruction with high expectations as much as a mainstream student (perhaps even more). Figure 5.10 lists additional findings from the National Reading Panel.

FIGURE 5.9

Vocabulary Chart

Word	Yes! I know the word well.	Not really! I have only seen or heard the word.	No way! I don't know the word.	I know the word and here is my definition.	This is a picture about the word.

FIGURE 5.10   National Reading Panel Recommendations

Suggestions for Vocabulary Development from the National Reading Panel

- Vocabulary can be learned incidentally by listening to others talk.
- Vocabulary can be learned by listening to stories read aloud.
- Students learn vocabulary by encountering words in various contexts.
- Teach vocabulary indirectly and directly.
- Rich classroom contexts enhance the acquisition of words.
- Direct instruction should actively engage the student.

Incidental Word Learning Through Read-Alouds

While it is important to provide direct vocabulary instruction during the day, the bulk of instruction in the language workshop is incidental word learning through teacher read-alouds. By talking about books, and reading aloud to children early and frequently, we will expand our students' vocabularies, and they will be better prepared for content instruction (Beck, McKeown, and Kucan 2002). This learning is enhanced by the direct instruction provided in the unit of study. In language workshop, units of study can be developed around genre, reading comprehension strategies, or content. Content is naturally abundant with specific words that we need to teach directly as well as indirectly through read-alouds and discussion (Lehr, Osborn, and Hiebert 2004).

Think of how rich the classroom would look, feel, and be! The teacher is reading aloud about a content area, focusing on the important parts to be learned in the text, using rich vocabulary from the content area while talking and leading a class discussion. Or, perhaps the teacher is reading aloud from a novel, noting reading comprehension strategies and student thinking on a chart while weaving in metacognitive vocabulary words like *reflect* and *analyze* and discussing words that appear in the text. The students are thinking, talking, writing, and warming up to using new words, exploring topics, or questioning texts. These activities help linguistic-minority students get a jump start at a level of literacy that mainstream students may already be involved in. This is so important because a student who is a good reader, who has lots of access to print, is involved in a reinforcing cycle of reading, learning new words because of reading, and understanding the teacher's vocabulary instruction. Language-minority students are much less likely to be on the same cycle (Cunningham and Stanovich 1998).

The language workshop focuses on moving struggling students quickly into instruction that reinforces this process. Specifically, during language workshop, vocabulary instruction is integrated in an activity that has multiple purposes. Integrating language acquisition and vocabulary development into rich classroom contexts is proven to work (Stahl and Nagy in press).

CHAPTER SIX

The Nuts and Bolts of Language Workshop

Now that you have an understanding of what language workshop can provide for your students, let's look at how you implement a workshop, what instruction supports the workshop, and why language workshop works.

How to Implement Language Workshop

Laurie leans forward, her face beaming. "You're right, Patricia, the giant wanted to help the village." She adds Patricia's thinking to the chart she has posted on the easel. "So, can you think of any other actions that we could write under *giant* on our chart?" Two students bob their heads together; Braulio points to a picture in the book in his lap and then moves his finger over to the words next to the picture. He talks with his partner and then shoots his hand in the air.

"Go ahead, Braulio, tell us your thinking."

"Well, I am thinking that the witch wants to help, too. I mean, see here on page 362, she goes to the giant and asks him, to . . . to cry. And if he cries he will help the village."

"OK, that isn't about the giant, but you are telling me that the witch wants to help also and that is important?"

"Yeah, I think you should write it down."

Laurie Cruz is leading a language workshop around the book *The Mysterious Giant of Barletta*, by Tomie dePaola (1988). The students are busy, thinking and conversing around the thoughts, actions, and feelings of two characters in the book, the giant and the witch. As they talk the room seems to burst with their energy; there are many language learners and linguistically diverse students in Laurie's class, but all of them are engaged. As I watch her lead, I too am drawn into the discussion. At one point I even pipe in with my thoughts about the giant's feelings. It is hard not to get swept up into the thinking and discussion. As I watch Laurie give the students time and opportunity to think about the characters' actions, thoughts, and feelings, I am struck by how many supports she places into her instruction and into her workshop. In the end, the group creates a list of character traits together.

I see many goals of language workshop in Laurie's instruction:

- Children share ideas, decisions, and understanding orally and in writing.
- Children carry on conversations with others about their thinking.
- Children are thinking critically by analyzing events in the book. They can also be involved in synthesizing, comparing, and evaluating texts, ideas, and problems.
- Children are learning to think critically by responding orally and in writing with peers and their teachers.
- Children are taught to reason by working together. Laurie's explicit instruction helps them become independent thinkers and learners.
- Children are learning to connect knowledge in thematic units of study.
- Children learn proper forms and functions of English through modeling.
- Children learn to be metacognitive thinkers, to think about their thinking and self-evaluate their learning.

These are not all of the things in place in Laurie's instruction, but these are critical structures Laurie has in place to focus on language development. Implementing language workshop isn't difficult, but it helps to understand the structure of the workshop and what thinking goes into the planning.

This is how to maintain comprehensible language during the language workshop. The teacher is:

- Reading aloud to the class
- Thinking aloud to unveil how the thinking process works
- Posing thoughtful questions to get the children delving into the big ideas around a book and related information
- Discussing the ideas presented in the book and the effect of the ideas on the characters and society

Language Workshop Features:

- Language workshop begins with a short minilesson (ten minutes maximum), which is followed by guided practice through a read-aloud.
- During the guided practice the group structure changes; students work in a large group, or in small groups, in pairs, or sometimes alone.
- The guided practice time is focused on *discussion.*
- During the guided practice the teacher reads aloud a literature book or nonfiction book, stopping at predetermined places to facilitate discussion.
- The minilesson and discussion is either a language lesson on *process* or on *structure.*

- While facilitating the discussion, the teacher purposefully pauses to give English learners time to process language and to respond independently or with a partner.
- During the discussion the teacher records information and ideas on charts, visuals, and sentence strips to give students time to process language and make the discussion comprehendible.
- Children in kindergarten through second grade learn to write about their ideas from the discussion through whole-class modeled writing. If ready, second graders can write responses in journals.
- Children in third through eighth grade learn to jot ideas down in response notebooks or journals.

Are you wondering what to keep in mind when planning your workshop? Begin by doing the following:

- Make your thinking transparent through modeling.
- Teach discourse skills through meaningful conversation.
- Focus on purposeful and authentic instruction and work.
- Give students multiple opportunities to have authentic conversations.
- Create a literate community in your classroom.
- Ensure that students write their thoughts and ideas in response notebooks and on charts.
- Focus appropriately on form and function of language.
- Accept student attempts to share and participate.

Components of the Workshop

There are two main structures to the language workshop:

1. minilesson (five to ten minutes)
2. guided practice during a read-aloud (twenty to thirty minutes)

During the guided practice the teacher reads aloud a fiction or nonfiction book and pauses in predetermined places to facilitate discussion. The discussion is based on the objective of the minilesson, which builds upon the overall goals of the current unit of study. The teacher writes and draws on charts, graphic organizers, sentence strips, or different sizes of paper to create visuals to aid discussion and comprehension of the discussion. The key is to write on things that are permanent and not erasable (like a whiteboard) because you will want to revisit the thoughts and graphics to add new ideas and information and clarify thinking, and you'll want to post the information as a reference to thinking and learning. The students may also write in journals or response notebooks.

What Happens During the Minilesson
The minilesson is the direct teaching time. The teacher presents a minilesson with four parts: connection, direct instruction, engagement, and closure (Calkins 2001). Now, let's looks at how these four parts look in the

language workshop. The following minilesson sequence is adapted from a lesson for writing workshop in my first book, *How to Align Literacy Instruction, Assessment, and Standards* (2004).

1. Connection (one minute)
- The teacher reminds students of what they have been learning on previous days in the current unit of study.
- She also discusses what they know as learners and thinkers in the classroom community.

   Strategy for Teaching English Learners:

- Tap into students' prior knowledge to remind them of what they have been learning.
- Connect this to the larger theme that is guiding their current work.

   Think of the example of Laurie's teaching at the beginning of the chapter. Laurie connected the children to the minilesson by saying: "We read *The Mysterious Giant of Barletta*, by Tomie dePaola the other day. And do you remember how we talked about what happened in the book?" (She pointed to a chart hanging nearby that listed the students' thinking about *The Mysterious Giant of Barletta*. "Well, the other day, during our discussion, many of you wanted to talk about the characters and why they were doing what they were doing. And guess what? Today, that is what we are going to do!"

2. Direct Instruction (five to six minutes)
- The teacher provides specific information about the day's new learning.
- This is not the time when the teacher poses questions to have the students recall information.
- She tells them what they are going to learn and why it is important to know this learning.

   Strategy for Teaching English Learners:

- Be explicit when teaching by using visuals, student models, charts, graphics, drawings, pictures, writing, and mentor texts.
- Explain how to break the thinking down into steps; show how this looks visually. Showcase student thinking to make the discussion understandable to the children acquiring English and for the children with less experience in thinking critically about ideas and information.

   In Laurie's lesson, she was explicit and supportive of the children during her teaching. She modeled how to think about character analysis by filling in the chart with her students and then discussing their thinking.

3. Engagement (one to two minutes)
- The teacher asks the children to think about the task for the day.
- She tells them to remind themselves of what they are going to do during the reading of the text.

Strategy for Teaching English Learners:

■ Have the students share with a partner, sitting knee to knee, eye to eye.
■ Ask the students to tell their partner what they are going to do during the read-aloud and discussion.
■ Have partners share information and discuss ideas cooperatively.

Laurie had the students think for a minute about the chart and what they knew about the characters in *The Mysterious Giant of Barletta*. She told them, "For just a minute I want you to think about the characters in the book and what you noticed about them when I read the book yesterday. Those are the things we are going to discuss." After a pause to give students time to think, Laurie continued. "Now, I want you to turn to your partner and tell your partner about what you remembered about some of the characters." Laurie paused, and then added, "Now tell your partner what we are going to do today while we read the book aloud again."

4. Closure (one minute)
■ The teacher strategically chooses a student or a paired group to share their thinking.
■ It is best if the teacher was listening to the quick discussion during the engagement so that she can strategically choose someone whose thinking will reinforce the lesson's goals.

Strategy for Teaching English Learners:

■ During the engagement part of the lesson, coach students so they'll be ready to share.
■ Encourage students who are acquiring English to share; don't overlook them.
■ Encourage students to point to the chart or visual from the lesson and use other gestures to help them communicate.

What Happens During the Guided Practice

This is a guided thinking and discussion that takes place while the teacher reads aloud from a fiction or literary nonfiction text. Sometimes the teacher may be revisiting a book previously read in order to discuss certain points from the book based on the current unit of study. It is important that the book be fiction or literary nonfiction so that there is depth and quality to the writing. For suggested book lists see Appendix B.

1. After the minilesson the teacher begins reading the book aloud. He has predetermined where he wants to stop to facilitate group work and discussion and has marked those spots with sticky notes. Perhaps the sticky notes even cue the teacher about what he needs to say (just so he doesn't forget).
2. The teacher reads to the first predetermined stopping point in the text and then poses a question for the group. While the children respond,

the teacher records their ideas on the chart that was started during the minilesson.

3. This sequence continues. The teacher reads a bit and then stops to facilitate discussion and jot notes on the chart, if appropriate.

4. Depending on the objective of the lesson, the teacher may have the students write about their thinking or fill in their own graphic organizers while revisiting a book with a partner. The organizer, titled Character Traits, Actions, and Effect or Plot Chart, Laurie gave her students is in Appendix A.

5. Have passion! This is the most important step. You can try language workshop, and follow all of these ideas, but if you aren't passionate about the ideas you are presenting, or passionate about the children you are teaching, your workshop won't be as successful as it could be. You can show passion in the following ways:

   - Exuding enthusiasm while reading and discussing the book.
   - Using voice inflection to reflect your feelings.
   - Being patient with children's responses and giving them the time they need to respond.
   - Displaying a love for the book you are using for the lesson *and sharing this feeling with the group!*
   - Showing an infatuation with the subject of a content study, *which, of course, you share with the students!*
   - Teaching slowly. It is true that the minilesson is very short, and I suggest twenty to thirty minutes for the workshop; however, being

FIGURE 6.1

Language Workshop Structure

Open with minilesson.
Follow the four parts of the minilesson: connection, direct instruction, engagement, and closure.

Begin reading.
Stop and discuss several times.
Stop and jot in language notebooks or on charts two to three times.
Ask: (1) "What are you thinking?" and (2) "Why?"

Move to groups.
Refocus to remind children of the minilesson (repeat the objective again).

Share at end.
Reinforce students or groups who did what you wanted them to do (regarding the objective of the minilesson).

Remember to focus on a slow way of teaching: Convey passion, give thinking time, and talk about the fine points of the book or issue.

---

rushed and stressed during this time is very different than teaching with care. To convey a passion for the book or subject, and to give English learners time to think, teach as if you had all the time in the world to think about this subject, talk about the fine points of the book, or discuss the author's thinking. You teach precisely in order to capture time for the luxuriousness of student thinking and classroom talk. You might get so carried away that the workshop lasts longer, but that's OK. I have often taught the language workshop for forty-five minutes to an hour. The time reference is only to help you fit language workshop into your day.

The Instruction That Supports the Workshop

Maya entered my office and gingerly sat on the edge of a chair. Accompanying her was David, who grabbed another chair and laid out an array of papers on my desk. "Look what we noticed," David said, pointing to some

FIGURE 6.2

Language Workshop Minilesson
(taught before beginning the day's reading)

Connection (1 minute):
Recap of previous day's reading and discussion.
Yesterday we read and discussed _____

Direct Instruction (5 minutes):
Teach, don't tell.
Show them how to think. Don't elicit responses here.
I noticed that when one person is speaking about her idea in the book, not all of us are listening to that person's ideas and then responding. We are too eager to just share our idea instead of listening. Let me show you how good readers have a book dialogue . . .

Engagement (1 minute):
Put your objective into short-term memory. You want your students to remember what to do right before they begin. This is a practice time for what they are supposed to do.
Turn to your partner and make a statement about the book. Your partner should listen and then respond, building upon what you said.

Closure (30 seconds to 1 minute):
Repeat the directive.
Today when I stop and pause, listen to what the person who's sharing is saying before you think of what you want to say. Good readers in a book dialogue listen to what the other people are saying before they formulate their ideas.

Then begin the reading.

---

student data on the papers scattered across my desk. "Maya and I had a hunch that if we talked more with students about what they thought were the big ideas in the content unit, the kids would retain the information better. See . . ." He pointed to a column of text scores. "We gave our end-of-unit social studies test, and they got it! Overall the kids understood more when we taught the content in the workshop."

"Wow, this is energizing!" I leaned forward to look at the students' increase in achievement scores from a previous test to the current test. "And how did your English learners do?"

"Just as well," David said and turned to Maya. She nodded.

"I am so excited. I was worried that combining the content with the language wouldn't be successful, but look! I think some of my kids, like Pao Yee, are speaking in English more often now too. I feel like her confidence grew."

David and Maya were thrilled with the information from their social studies quiz because they knew and understood what they were asking the students to do in language and in content, and they saw results. It is important to grasp what instruction supports the language workshop. Some of the instruction has roots in philosophical approaches of teaching English as a second language. When you know and recognize these approaches, planning for instruction makes more sense, and you are grounding your teaching in well-practiced methods. Let's look at the two philosophical approaches of second language instruction that support effective teaching in the workshop: the communicative approach and the cognitive approach (Herrera and Murray 2005). The language workshop incorporates both approaches. This is important to realize because you will balance your instruction between communication and cognitive processes. Both are important, and one doesn't outweigh the other. When we focus on communication, we are expecting students to acquire language through interaction, cooperative learning, and talk. When we focus on cognitive (or thinking) processes, we are facilitating lessons where students acquire language by thinking of their thinking and focusing on strategies to use when reading and writing.

The Communicative Approach
The communicative approach is student centered and emphasizes acquisition of knowledge and communication. Three well-known methods of the communicative approach include the natural approach, integrated content-based instruction, and sheltered instruction. These methods are widely practiced and may be familiar to you from English language development training or classes.

Sheltered instruction (Echevarria and Graves 2002; Freeman and Freeman 1998) includes

- grade-level-modified content instruction
- scaffolded instruction

- use of visuals
- cooperative learning
- simplified vocabulary

The natural approach (Chamot and O'Malley 1994; Herrera and Murray 2005; Krashen 2003) includes

- comprehensible input
- minimal error correction
- acceptance of students' first language use
- content-based instruction (sometimes)
- lessons organized around activities and topics of interest

Integrated content-based instruction (Crandall 1994; Herrera and Murray 2005) includes

- language learning through content
- focus on the integration of content
- subjects taught in themes

The Cognitive Approach

The cognitive approach is a newer approach. It originated in the 1980s and 1990s and developed out of research on learning, memory, and cognition. This approach is also learner centered, but the focus is heavily organized around explicit teaching of learning strategies for communication (Herrera and Murray 2005; Chamot and O'Malley 1994). Current reading research supports cognitive methods in teaching reading comprehension skills. These cognitive skills, or comprehension skills, help students understand information and ideas in English, help them improve their reading ability, and teach students to be metacognitive. In plain terms, the cognitive approach helps students focus on their thoughts and their learning. The best-known method for the cognitive approach is CALLA (Chamot and O'Malley 1993). Some highlights of the CALLA method include

- developmental language instruction
- focus on academic language and content knowledge in both the first and the second language
- explicit instruction in metacognitive strategies
    - focusing on prior knowledge
    - planning a purpose for reading
    - self-monitoring comprehension
    - self-assessing how well one met the goal for reading

Process and Structure Lessons Revisited

Think about the two types of language instruction that I introduced in Chapter 3; these two prongs are the *processes* through which we acquire language, and the *structures* that we acquire. It is important to be aware of designing lessons that focus on learning processes and lessons that focus on learning structures. If we overrely on one prong or the other, students'

FIGURE 6.3 Two Prongs of Language Instruction

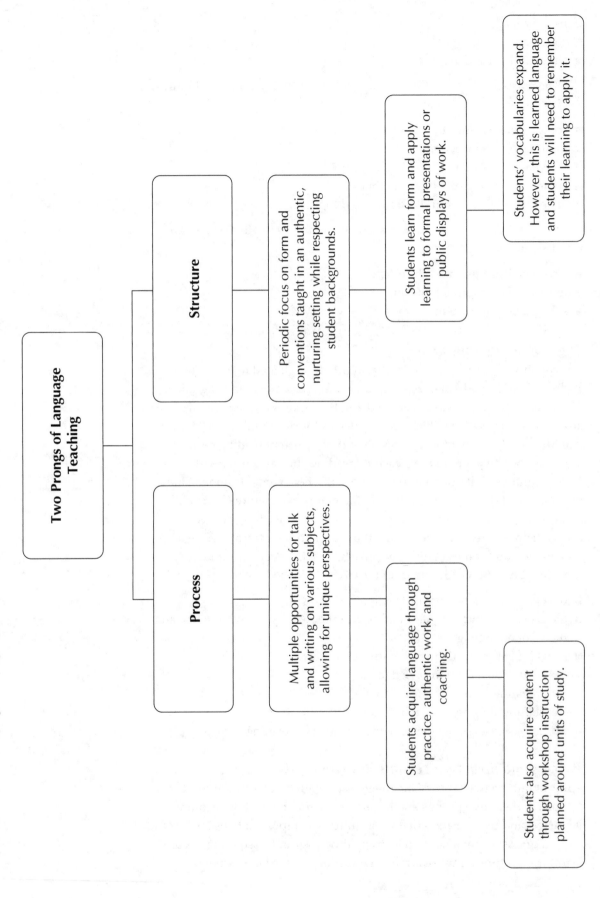

Two Prongs of Language Teaching

Process

Multiple opportunities for talk and writing on various subjects, allowing for unique perspectives.

Students acquire language through practice, authentic work, and coaching.

Students also acquire content through workshop instruction planned around units of study.

Structure

Periodic focus on form and conventions taught in an authentic, nurturing setting while respecting student backgrounds.

Students learn form and apply learning to formal presentations or public displays of work.

Students' vocabularies expand. However, this is learned language and students will need to remember their learning to apply it.

language learning will not be maximized. In Figure 6.3 you can see these lessons graphed as two prongs of your language workshop. The prong on the left shows the classroom processes through which students use language to acquire language, the prong on the right shows a few of the structures students should focus on in order to prepare for more formal classroom discourses.

Cazden (2001) describes this two-prong approach to instruction. She states that one prong should give students multiple opportunities to participate in authentic conversations and writing in order to help them be literate and become part of a literate community in your classroom. The second prong includes a periodic focus on conventions of form, taught as cultural conventions that you expect students to use during public presentations or for particular audiences. Remember that students need to be explicitly taught discourse skills and literacy. But *how* you teach this is important.

In the language workshop the precise instruction in the minilesson, and the opportunity to talk, think, and write, is where we make our teacher thinking transparent. This is why this type of instruction supports language workshop. Authentic conversation and the periodic instruction of form need to be provided in purposeful, authentic ways (Cazden 2001). The students need to talk, and talk often; it isn't purposeful to fill the students' time with tasks like worksheets. Students need to be actively engaged, and the use of worksheets should shift to the use of graphic organizers to help students think and record information (Hernández 2003). As language teachers, we have to provide the necessary support for students learning English through excellent, scaffolded instruction (Hale 2004).

Classroom Talk Supports Language Workshop

Classroom talk is important! Your workshop should not be a quiet time of day. During the guided practice portion of the lesson, your students are talking, and you are talking. At times it might be downright noisy in your room! This is wonderful and exciting; it means that your students are acquiring language. Many times I have sat with a group of children on the floor of their classroom and been amazed by the conversations going on around a book or idea. Your workshop should feel vibrant and alive.

Classroom talk assumes greater importance in the workshop; the children learn content and acquire language through interaction and discussion. In order to foster classroom talk, and be effective, it is important to accept student dialects and attempts at English in order to reinforce opportunities for students to build on the language they bring to school (Anderson and Barnitz 1998; Barnitz 1998; Christian 1997). The second prong (structure lessons), shown in Figure 6.3, emphasizes teaching the forms and functions of language, but this doesn't mean we should reduce the importance of a student's native language or dialect. We need to value the student's abilities but teach expected discourses for particular audiences (Cazden 2001). For instance, when children are speaking aloud, giving a presentation, or putting the final touches on written work for publication, they need to know how the work should sound or look. I often teach these structures during conferences with students or when using mentor texts. I want to support their background, and their developmental level, but I also want them to develop an understanding of presentation voice and published writing.

Why Language Workshop Works

Language workshop works because language is acquired most effectively when used for a real purpose. Communication in the workshop is meaningful and occurs in socially significant situations, which is that wonderful classroom talk through guided practice (Barnitz 1998; Snow, Met, and Genesee 1989). In the workshop, content instruction is often tied intrinsically to our students' desire to learn, and the interesting content propels their motivation. So remember:

1. Language is integrated with content.
2. Whole-group and small-group work is focused on important talk.

FIGURE 6.4　Instruction That Supports Language Workshop

Language Workshop

During Reading:

- Unpack your thinking out loud. Show your thinking; don't tell your opinions.
- Pose questions to make the kids think. Have them write notes around their thinking and around the direction you are leading in the book (character, plot, theme, action, etc.). Jot:

    What are you thinking?

    Why?

    What makes you think that? (action/event in the book)

    What are you connecting that idea to in the book/nonfiction text?

- Don't recap what the kids say. Focus on having them listen to the person who's speaking and then build the conversation on the last person's comments. Focus on the building of conversation, not having them get their own idea out without reflecting on what others have said.
- Let them state their thought, and then model the reflection. The students need to talk!

Discuss:

Does anyone agree?

Does anyone disagree?

Does that remind anyone of something in the book, another book, or a situation?

_____, what do you think about what _____ said?

---

3. The focus is on high-level thinking and problem solving. The teacher plans for it in order to make it happen.

The workshop focuses on

- communication
- socially significant lessons
- connections to literature and literary nonfiction
- content instruction planned around themed units of study

The workshop instruction improves student ability because of the authentic interaction and purposeful instruction, but you can also teach vocabulary and academic language structures through interactive group activities. Some important strategies students should learn include summarizing, analyzing, evaluating, composing, interpreting ideas, gleaning information from charts, graphs, and pictures, and determining what is important information in texts (Wong Fillmore and Snow 2000; Dutro and Moran 2003).

Language Workshop Teaches Cognitive and Metacognitive Strategies

Children lack experience in thinking like adults, so we have to model thinking for them and give them ways to try this thinking out (Pearson and Duke 2002; Jimenez, Garcia, and Pearson 1996). I often see mainstream students come to school prepared to think, evaluate, question, and synthesize. Many of these students come to school ready to think like this because they have had practice at dinner-table conversations or are lucky enough to have someone talk and think with them at home. I believe that all students need to know how to think, question, and then state their ideas well publicly, so in the language workshop we give students the opportunity to develop these skills (Delpit 1989; Avalos 2003).

Remember that during the guided practice portion of the workshop, the teacher reads the text aloud and then facilitates a discussion. This encourages the construction of meaning as students develop their understanding and attempt to use new vocabulary to express their ideas (Avalos 2003). Through interacting and your guidance, the children use cues from the text and their background knowledge to comprehend text, understand the conversation, and acquire language (Freeman and Freeman 2003). The workshop gives children the opportunity to learn how to think, and to evaluate their learning, and it motivates them to learn more.

Why a Workshop?

A workshop setting impacts the cognitive development of English learners and linguistically diverse students. Piaget referred to the structures in our brain that hold information as schemata (Hernández 2003). When students learn, our schemata is reorganized to adjust to the new information. This includes new language, strategies, or structures of language. In language workshop students' neurons are firing because they are in an active mode, and not passively listening to the teacher. They are given time and experiences to develop new schemata, or to reorganize existing structures to acquire new language and understand concepts. So, by providing English language development in a workshop structure, you are encouraging brain development and language acquisition.

When you plan the curriculum in your language workshop, you can organize units of study that build upon one another. (See Chapter 8 for more on how to plan units.) These units should be organized around content goals, language goals, and genre goals (Hernández 2003). The units should also be organized around fostering complex thinking. Thinking and problem solving are dependent on language skills. If we are not proficient in a language, it is hard to express ourselves in writing or to orally describe, defend, or share our ideas. In language workshop you have the opportunity to foster language acquisition, and give students practice thinking. It is really important that we develop students' ability to use oral and written language to think critically and communicate effectively.

In the workshop you can help your students contribute information, rather than just receive information. This supports students' backgrounds, differences of opinions, ability to provide purpose to the classroom community, and ways of interacting with peers. When we focus our language workshop around books and content, rather than worksheets or isolated vocabulary drills, we are not only developing literacy but closing an achievement gap that exists between affluent students and students of poverty (Daniels and Zemelman 2003; Olsen and Jaramillo 1999). Culturally and linguistically diverse students need instruction that is

- explicit
- intensive
- engaging
- supportive (Torgesen 2004)

Language workshop is a way to bridge the gap. Language workshop also bridges the achievement gap by presenting instruction in pedagogically sound ways.

- Language workshop gives students opportunities to think, share, work in groups, and problem solve in a number of ways, much like Laurie's class in the beginning of the chapter. By combining the oral and written language teaching with critical thinking through an organized inquiry around a read-aloud, Laurie focused on authentic ways for students to gather information and share their ideas.
- Language workshop gives students opportunities to speak and initiate language. This is important because students learning language often don't have multiple ways to say things, or argue a point, or develop

vocabulary. Without practice they develop inappropriate and incorrect language models.

- Language workshop is an environment that supports learning, promotes purposeful activities, and encourages exploration of language and thought within interdisciplinary themes.

CHAPTER SEVEN

Conferring

Essential Teaching and Assessment

As I write, my daughter sleeps. A few minutes ago I left her in her dark room; she was settled underneath a layer of blankets. Often at night, just as I am tucking her in, she runs down a long list—just as she did tonight—of things she wants me to remember. These things keep her connected to me and her daytime world just as she slips into sleep. Usually her list includes a question about homework, a reminder about the permission slip for an upcoming field trip, or a request for what she longs to have in her lunch box the next day. Tonight, in the moment just before she slipped into sleep, she murmured, "Don't forget I have word masters too."

"I remember."

"Oh, and I need my sweatshirt." Her voice was barely audible, drifting off.

"I remember." I kissed her forehead and hair and turned out the light.

These moments, where in the dark she reminds me of things important to her, of things she needs, of things I need to do to help her be successful, help me understand the next steps I need to take to help my daughter grow. These are the things I take mental notes of and then honor the next day in a way that doesn't just meet my daughter's needs but also teaches her and supports her next step.

Students also send me similar subtle signals during the day. In the lunch line a child might whisper, "Tomorrow is my birthday," or "I didn't read my book last night." When I happen by their classrooms, and see these messages in their writing or their reading, I informally assess student strengths and needs. Students tell us things all day, but most of the time we are so busy running our classrooms that we don't notice all of the signals and information we can gather in order to teach well. We have to learn how to assess and collect this information.

Once we know, understand, and control the subject of what our students need to know, we apply this knowledge to assess our students. With our own background knowledge, and an understanding of our students' knowledge, we know what to teach. Then it is easy to develop precise, focused lessons with accompanying rubrics that students can use to self-assess, that teachers can use to evaluate student learning and products, and that parents can use in order to be involved in their children's growth and development.

The teacher instructs, but the teacher is also the coach—the person on the sideline showing the student the way, giving encouragement, and picking up the student when he falls down. This is hard to do for 180 days non-stop with all sorts of personalities and ability levels in a classroom. How does the teacher accomplish this?

1. Students ask questions of themselves and their work.
Students should consider their writing and reading work in the workshops and ask, "What am I understanding of this? How can I make my work better? If my favorite author writes a beginning with a surprise, can I try that? Do the character actions affect the plot? Why did the author create a character I don't like, or one I love?"

The list of questions and ideas could go on and on. By encouraging student thinking and engagement with material, the teacher encourages continued motivation through learning. When the teacher knows what needs to be taught, and the students understand what they need to do in small steps and can understand how to improve their learning, they stay motivated.

Questioning is developed and encouraged through:

- Use of visuals in minilessons—Recording key ideas presented in mini-lessons on chart paper creates a visual large enough for the whole class to see, provides authentic examples, and sets the tone for the discussion. The charts also make the learning and thinking (the metacognitive process of thinking about thinking) transparent. The charts stand as references for students.
- Discussion—Students at all language ability levels discuss their thinking in all workshops, but specifically in language workshop. The point is for the teacher to coach students to think and talk. It is their thinking that is correct, not the teacher's interpretation. The teacher guides, cajoles, encourages, and nudges.
- Writing—The use of response journals in all workshops develops self-evaluation, reflection, and awareness of knowledge and understanding. When writing, students may discover they know more than they thought, understand something by having to explain it, or identify areas where they need help or clarification.

2. Students understand how to improve their work through mentor texts.
Many times children think that writers and thinkers spring from bed each morning bursting with ideas on their own. They don't realize that writers

and thinkers learn from each other. They probably also don't realize how much their parents, on the job or in the home, learn from mentors. Studying mentor texts teaches children to

- Read like a writer
- Unpack writing for the techniques that are evident within it
- Try out the techniques in their own writing
- Turn to class members to help them comprehend reading
- Engage in discourse with peers in which they learn to listen and learn from what a peer is saying
- Set learning goals and visualize a model of good work

3. The teacher provides precise lessons focused on the needs of the learner and the expected grade-level curriculum.
The teacher is there every day, creating a classroom full of books and interesting texts to read and think about. The teacher coaches from the side, giving suggestions to children when they cannot quite figure out a word or understand the meaning. The teacher is there to give the child another book to read, and another and another. The teacher's role is to support the child in becoming an independent, self-reliant reader and thinker (Goodman 2003).

It is important to help students make meaning of information they read and discuss. Making meaning is more than processing individual words; keep in mind what good readers do when tackling a text. These are the same behaviors to encourage in language workshop. As students focus in language workshop, it helps to let the groups have one or more copies of the book to facilitate the discussions. When students make meaning in language workshop, they may

- Read from the beginning to the end of the text, although they jump around, look ahead, and look back
- Process information related to their goal for the text
- Anticipate what might be in the text based on their prior knowledge of the topic
- Monitor their comprehension and develop the ability to determine what information is important for comprehension as they read
- Recognize which parts of the text are vague or confusing
- Reflect on what they read; they might interpret how the ideas could impact their lives or how they might use the information

Linking Conferring with Assessment

The best way to assess student language development quickly every day is through conferring. Most often we assess student needs in reading, writing, and language while conferring during reading workshop and writing workshop. We can also confer during language workshop; however, since time may be limited, you may confer with students only in groups. Not only does this help you gain information about who is participating, talking, and sharing ideas, but it helps you keep the groups on track.

The outcomes of conferring in language workshop should complement your instruction and student work in reading and writing workshop. While there are differences in conferring between the workshops, talking for a few moments, gathering information about your students, and helping them stay on track is important for assessment and coaching.

Conferring goals in language workshop include

- Ensuring all students are talking (not letting one student dominate)
- Checking group understanding of the discussion topic
- Watching to see if students are using graphics, charts, and knowledge about books to help them discuss
- Helping students reflect together and come up with an idea about a topic or discussion point
- Helping students organize, evaluate, and synthesize information
- Assessing students' oral language ability

The goals in language workshop often complement goals for reading workshop. In reading workshop children learn to read through focused instruction in minilessons, guided reading, and strategy lessons. They spend large amounts of time reading texts at the reading level around content of interest. Another component of reading workshop is the time children spend responding to their reading with partners and individually, both orally and in writing. Conferring goals in reading workshop include

- Supporting student learning
- Reteaching objectives from minilessons
- Assessing student learning
- Encouraging independent reading
- Encouraging sustainability (reading for long periods of time)
- Developing reflective and self-evaluative learners
- Coaching comprehension strategies
- Teaching the students to think; they should own the learning

When we confer in reading, we observe student ability in

- just right books
- instructional texts
- use of fix-up strategies
- comprehension development
- desire to read
- ability to discuss books

When we confer in language workshop, we observe students' ability to reflect on their learning. Successful students pose questions before reading, are metacognitive, and show greater improvements in school than students who are unengaged and not self-reflective. Students might ask:

- What am I trying to accomplish?
- What choices help me with my reading or writing?
- What strategies help me become a better reader or writer?
- How well do my choices (craft, strategy) match what I want to accomplish?
- How do I feel about my work and my process?

Because of the length of the language workshop, there isn't a lot of time for individual conferring as in reading and writing workshop. Therefore, the teacher should be walking around the class and checking in with groups of students while they're having a discussion writing their ideas down for future discussion.

Conferring in Language Workshop

Sue Shollenbarger laid the book *Two Bear Cubs: A Miwok Legend from California's Yosemite Valley*, by Robert D. San Souci (1997), in her lap. She took her reading glasses off, folded them, and laid them in her lap. For a moment, she looked at each one of her students, making eye contact with them as they settled with their partners on the floor.

"We have been reading about different Indian fables, and we have been thinking about the characters in our reading and how their characteristics affect the story. Look at the chart behind me. We have listed several things that have happened in the fables we have read so far. Today we are going to read and discuss the characters, which are bears, in this book." Sue held the book *Two Bear Cubs* up. "These bears get themselves into a predicament. There is one character who ends up solving the problem the other characters have. I am going to add a column to our chart, and we need to think about who is the hero, or the one who solves the problems, in the fables we read."

Sue flipped the chart pad to a clean sheet and wrote: "Main character," "Problem," and "Character Who Solves Problem." She went on to discuss each heading on the chart. "Now, before we read our book for today, I want you to talk with your partner and discuss what character solved the problem in *Bear Dreams. Bear Dreams* is the book we read yesterday." Sue flipped to one of the last pages in the book and swept her hand over the picture. "Yesterday we talked about the bear and the tribe, and we listed some of the traits on the chart, but we didn't talk about the boy and how his character traits helped him, or *enabled* him, to solve the tribe's problem." Sue placed the chart from the previous day's lesson on the easel and then reminded her fourth graders of what they were to discuss. A buzz emerged from the group; the students quickly became engaged with their partners.

It was at this point that Sue first conferred with students during the language workshop. She was still presenting her minilesson—which was on having students analyze how the character traits of the hero helped him or her solve the problem in a fable—but she stopped here for two or three minutes in order to tap knowledge from a previous lesson and to have the students think about the character and the traits on their own. While they talked among themselves, she listened in on one group's conversation. Then she continued the lesson. "Many of you were engaged talking with your partners about the traits of the boy; he saved the tribe by being brave. I just talked with Brianda's group. Brianda, Juan, and Mark thought about the boy and thought about what traits helped him solve the problem. Brianda, would your group come up and share your thinking with the class?" Sue called the group she had conferred with to the front in order to unpack their thinking with the class. She used their thinking process as a model for the class.

The students shared their thinking and Sue wrote on the chart. "Brianda's group stated that the boy was brave and thoughtful and these traits helped him on his journey to bring the bear back to the tribe. They also stated that he didn't give up. I wrote the word *persevere*, which means not to give up easily, on the chart. I also added that he persevered because the trip was difficult. It was hard for him to find the bear."

Sue had the group sit down. "Today when we are reading, we are going to think about the character traits of the hero, the animal or person who solves the problem, and we are going to write our new thinking on our chart. Remember, the traits of the characters make them interesting and give us clues about what might happen in the story while we are reading."

Sue then began the read-aloud portion of the language workshop. When she stopped to facilitate discussion, she focused on getting students to think for themselves and recording their thoughts on the chart. She also encouraged them to listen to one another and build on the ideas presented by other students. During this active engagement, she moved from whole-group discussion to small-group discussion. When the small groups talked and worked together, she moved among the groups and conferred with one or two groups to ensure that the students were engaged and on track.

When We Confer

When we confer we illuminate how something is to be done in conversation, in thinking, in writing, or in reading. We teach children how thinking looks, how talking should sound, within a precise conversation around one or two points; we give students immediate feedback. The focus of conferring in language workshop is to help students participate in academic conversation around literary or content goals. We have to focus on what we want students to do and how instruction and student participation should look in our classrooms. Developing this focus consists of knowing our teaching steps, understanding student performance, and knowing what student products should look like. Performance is the process of what students do, think, and create in our rooms. Products are what they create.

1. Think of the next teaching step:
   ■ Is the child participating?

- Is the child ready to lead a group discussion?
- Is the child using strategies to participate in discussion?
- Does the child comprehend the discussion?
- Is the child acquiring language and developing the ability to talk about books, talk about his thinking, and listen to his partner's ideas?
- Does the child jot ideas down in his language response notebook? Does he jot notes on sticky notes?

2. Think of student performance. Does the student know
   - How words work?
   - How print works?
   - How text structure works?
   - How to remember?
   - How to talk about her ideas?

3. Think of the student product:
   - Does the child keep up-to-date notes, jots, brain dumps? (see Akhavan 2004, 204)
   - Does the child finish literary responses in writing workshop using notes from language workshop?
   - Does the child speak in large groups?
   - Does the child participate in small-group discussion?

Research-Based Practices That Guide Conferences

I have often been asked if conferring with students is worthwhile. I cannot imagine not conferring with students; this is an opportunity to assess the value of my teaching and understand what my students have learned. When someone asks me, "Is this teaching researched based?" I answer with a resonant *yes*.

Research by Marzano, Pickering, and Pollack (2001) shows several specific practices that work well in classrooms and support student learning. I have naturally built these practices into my conferences over time. Following are the six points in Marzano, Pickering, and Pollack's research that apply to conferring:

- Students need immediate feedback.
- Effort should be reinforced.
- Students need practice.
- Practice should point out pitfalls and errors.
- Practice should model correct action.
- Practice helps a student master a process or skill.

Willingham (2004) adds that practice should be differentiated based on the importance of the strategy to the content taught. I also believe it is important to differentiate practice based on the developmental level and acquisition needs of the students.

When I confer I am giving students immediate feedback, and reinforcing effort during a structured practice time during the workshop.

Discussing a topic with a peer is practice, jotting notes in a language note-book is practice, talking your ideas out is practice. In all of these instances, the child is the active thinker, and I am the observer. Then if I notice that a child is off track, not participating, or not understanding, I gently redirect the student. I do this through questioning: "Tell me why . . . ," "What are you thinking about . . . ?" "Have you tried . . . ?" I also provide support: "Do you remember when I talked about my thinking . . . ?" "Look at the chart we wrote yesterday, the chart lists . . . ," "I notice you wrote about your idea, but can you write about *why* you think that. Use the chart from yesterday's language workshop to help you think about . . ." When I confer I also notice if a child is on track. Then, if the child needs to be nudged for-ward a bit, I tell him what he did that was correct and offer suggestions to help him think deeper, explain more, or discuss further. I might say, "Wow, you wrote a lot about your thinking. Can you add more in the column on examples of . . . ?" or "I noticed that you and your partner talked through everything quickly; what else do you think about . . . ? Can you talk about that too?" or "The way that you explained yourself is clear, and I can tell you have been thinking a lot about this topic, but what do you think about . . . ?"

Conferring is a time to assess and reteach information, strategies, and concepts to a student individually. When I confer, I listen. When I confer, I act. I am intent on what the *student* can tell me about her learning. I watch very carefully what the child can do on her own, without my support; then I observe and prod a bit to see what the child cannot do without support. It is that point which I choose to teach or use to push the student; I might describe a concept again, provide a strategy, or demonstrate.

Student and Teacher Responsibilities During Conferences

Remember that we confer to assess, guide, model, and reteach. However, conferring is instruction that begins with the child telling us what he is doing, explaining his thinking, and perhaps showing us his writing about his thinking. The conference begins with me asking the student to explain and to open up. I want the student to do the thinking and to be prepared to think about his thinking. I might begin the conference by asking, "How is it going?" "What are you talking about?" "Tell me what you think," or "What are you working on?"

It is after I open the conference that the responsibility shifts to the stu-dent. That is when I listen carefully for what the child is able to do without support and what I need to model or suggest the child try to do on his own. I am providing direct individualized instruction that nudges a student into his zone of proximal development. The zone of proximal development is the learning point. The child isn't overwhelmed with information and frus-trated, but the task isn't so easy that the work is effortless. Learning occurs when a child is given a task that is just beyond what she can do alone (Vy-gotsky 1980). When conferring, if I notice a child is frustrated, I offer sup-port to reduce frustration and make sure the child is learning. I might change or restate an assignment; I might regroup students to work with different partners or place more students in one group; I might point out a visual or contextual support in the classroom. I focus on giving the child the language to do the current task through:

- minilessons
- charts describing process
- charts showing the class' thinking
- books, pictures, maps, and so on
- modeling

At this point, the responsibility shifts back to the student. I ask the student what he is going to do next; I focus on making sure the child is clear and has a goal for his next steps. During conferences I want both the teacher and the student to be responsible for the learning. We both have a part in what is occurring even if the conference lasts just a couple of minutes.

Teacher responsibilities include

- knowing your students well through assessment
- setting goals based on student skills and the unit of study
- providing feedback and encouragement
- helping students become metacognitive

Student responsibilities include

- showing effort
- focusing on goals
- reflecting on progress
- making decisions to improve learning
- participating in group discussions
- writing about their thinking

Conferring Keeps Us on Track

Conferring is important in language workshop because we need to know what our students can do in order to offer appropriate guidance and support. Most often students are giving us subtle messages: notice this, I cannot do this, I need help, if you only would . . . These are some of the messages that children send to us silently. Unmotivated and struggling learners aren't going to come forth and tell you these things; you have to take the time to notice and then teach. When we confer, we build a routine that gives us the time to notice these things every day.

Conferring is important, but it is easy to lose track of the focus. Keep yourself on track by focusing on four steps in conferring.

1. **Know where you are going.**

- Hold your instruction accountable.
- Keep anecdotal notes on student progress.

2. Know your students well.

- Use formal and informal assessment to make coaching decisions.
- Coach your students.
- Remind them of their goals.
- Remind them of strategies that work.
- Prod them to apply themselves while giving encouragement.

3. Be supportive and enthusiastic.

- They will learn to love reading and writing from you.
- They learn from what we model, not from what we say.

4. Set a goal.

- Give them the wings to practice a bit without you.

PART THREE

Units of Study in Content and Strategy

CHAPTER EIGHT

Putting It All Together

How to Develop Units of Study That Link Language, Reading, and Writing

Ronique tapped her pencil on the table as she pondered how to add conferring into her overpacked teaching day. (Refer to Chapter 7 for a discussion on conferring and assessment.) "I just don't get it—where am I supposed to fit conferring into my schedule? What am I supposed to give up?"

"Well, we need to think of it as not giving up something, but organizing our day into a coherent schedule where what we do during the day connects," I answered as I took a seat at her table. Ronique was working with a group of three teachers at a daylong inservice; the group was focused on adding purposeful assessment into the language arts instruction.

"Umph." She paused. "Well, I still don't get it; I just cannot seem to wrap my mind around how to fit these things together. As I think of all the things I am supposed to do during the day, the whole idea of creating a purposeful and authentic classroom, while ensuring that I meet students' language needs, and having rigorous content . . . well, it is just overwhelming." Ronique threw her hands in the air. "I mean, I like it, don't get me wrong. But how do I even begin to think about it?"

How do we begin to think about organizing instruction? In just a short discussion Ronique summed up the purpose for our meeting that day and the question that teachers often pose to me. *How do we begin to organize all that we know to be important for diverse students?* The answer isn't simple and there isn't a silver bullet program to solve the dilemma for us, but it certainly begins with planning. For too many years I lugged home fifty pounds of teachers manuals and pored over them, carefully and dutifully copying my plans into my lesson plan book. I hoped that my lessons had rigor, but I never had a gauge to measure the expectations I planned for student learning. I often worried that my targets were too low, that I was dumbing down the curriculum just to get through it, or that possibly, because I didn't understand how to teach a particular subject, I wasn't expecting enough of students. When we plan well, using standards, our prior knowledge, and grade-level expectations as a guide, we can improve the rigor of our instruction.

Desired Results

Each August I am amazed by the amount of information that falls upon a teacher's doorstep. In addition to the expectations for teachers beyond their classroom including cocurricular and school governance issues, teachers are weighed down with yard duty schedules, special team meetings, and several back-to-school reminders from administrators. Sometimes amid the issues and management directives, the curriculum gets lost. Usually we find our curriculum guides shoved on dusty shelves, and reading these guides doesn't shed light onto the ever burning question: What should I teach the first month of school, the first week—OK, be realistic—what do I teach on the first day?

As we gain expertise, we put our classrooms and curriculum together like a mosaic, fitting in state and district expectations and layering in our own personal knowledge and expectations for what we love to teach. The movement toward standards-based education at best helps align our work to what students should know and be able to do at a grade level and at worst fills pages of a teacher manual that we follow mindlessly. The most powerful thing we can do for ourselves, our colleagues, and our students is to take the time to sit down together and plan our days, our months, and our year.

When planning it is important to focus on what the students need to know and be able to do at each grade level. State and national standards list this information, but we still have to translate it into a meaningful curriculum and into an authentic, purposeful teaching day. A teacher has the greatest impact upon the content that students will be exposed to in any given year. The content should go beyond what you are comfortable presenting and include information from

- professional development texts
- standards
- grade-level expectations
- district and state curriculum guidelines
- content that meets the needs of your students
- publishers' guidelines

As discussed in previous chapters, desired results for language learners include competency in various discourse patterns, acquisition of English, which is fostered in language workshop, and literacy, which is nurtured in reading and writing workshops. While thinking of all the components of an effective language development classroom can be overwhelming, it is important to get a handle on each component and plan carefully for implementation.

Units of Study

Let's begin by picturing three children reading a book silently, sitting side by side, with notebooks in their laps. They are just sitting there, reading, and from time to time stopping to write a note in their notebooks. Occasionally, one child smiles, and nods his head, and then he quickly writes a note in his notebook. He is having a silent conversation with his book. Another student turns a page, looks up to see what his partners are doing, and then focuses back on his book. It is a serene picture, the students' knees almost touching, the quiet rhythm of breathing punctuated by the occasional sound of a page turning. It is a gratifying picture, because we know that inside the children's heads they are wrapped inside a story that the author is telling them as they read. It is a voice that only they can hear, perhaps accompanied by their own voice as they ponder and consider the events in the story or the character's actions. With the book in hand, it is an adventure that only they can have, but soon each child will turn to his partners and share his experience.

The silent, motionless activity of reading is soon punctuated with a murmur of three students talking about what they just read. Soon, each group finishes reading and the murmur becomes louder, peppered with phrases soaring above the din, "I know, I know . . . I think the author meant . . ." The teacher's voice, deeper and insistent, prods one group. His voice is melodic and mixed in with the rise and fall of the children's voices. "Let's think about that a little bit more; you are telling me that . . ."

As the children sat motionless with books in hand, they were comprehending what they were reading and noting their ideas in journals, based on modeling from their teacher. They were simultaneously comprehending text while analyzing the focus their teacher posed in a minilesson. The students were well versed in how to talk with one another about their books, and their discussions challenged and prodded each other's thinking. In discussion, they explored concepts, ideas, events, and actions. This connection and engagement, including the ability to critically evaluate ideas, texts, and issues and discuss them well, is what students involved in language workshop should be able to experience.

As noted in the first part of the book, there are many factors to incorporate into language instruction. We have to consider the language ability of the child, her acquisition level, vocabulary development focused on level two words, the atmosphere in our rooms, regular opportunities for sustained thinking and discussion, and opportunities for students to hear text read aloud.

By focusing our curriculum into units of study, it is possible to plan authentic and powerful curriculum that meets the needs of diverse learners while affording us the opportunity to teach to grade-level expectations and standards. Units of study are plans that extend over time and have a thematic focus on a specific comprehension strategy or context study. A unit creates a comprehensive learning opportunity for all students in your classroom. Units of study build like blocks, one upon the other, as you organize teaching and assess learning throughout the year.

- Units set a purpose for instruction.
- Units guide instruction.
- Units organize assessment from instruction.
- Units define student products and processes.

When we plan and deliver instruction through focused units of study, our focus helps us achieve the desired results in our classroom. We want to develop the unit around inquiry, discussion, and language; however, it is important to ensure that instruction is directed at standards or grade-level expectations (these may also be considered core content). Therefore, a unit

- Creates an engaging learning experience for students by emphasizing students' thinking and their application of learning and connecting learning to their lives
- Becomes an organized plan to guide instruction and assessment
- Focuses on what is most important for students to know and be able to do
- Embeds a variety of experiences in reading, writing, and oral language across the curriculum
- Addresses ways to meet students' individual needs

Teaching Resources

The last two chapters of the book provide sample units of study organized by theme, by genre, and by specific strategies. The units help students connect to an inquiry by organizing minilessons by issues and topics addressed in a theme. A unit on strategies can be organized with minilessons explicitly teaching how to use various strategies, and how good readers and thinkers use strategies to understand and comprehend. Other units organize information by having students examine writing genres, unpack authors' thinking, and then apply this information to books they read. In these units we aren't teaching predetermined facts; we are posing an inquiry focused on critical thinking and developing in-depth knowledge. The heart of an inquiry unit should be focused on personal and social knowledge. The children bring knowledge they gain from their own experiences of living in their world and apply this knowledge to the theme or topic discussed. The students have background knowledge from their specific cultural groups and from their neighborhoods (Short, Harste, and Burke 1996). The inquiry begins with what they know, think, and feel and builds upon their knowledge, helping them learn language, broaden their background knowledge, and develop cognitive elements like language comprehension and critical thinking (Wren 2000).

The units of study for language workshop are not taught in isolation from instruction in the other workshops. The focus of a unit of study can expand across reading and writing workshops. While this isn't always desirable, when teaching a specific comprehension strategy as the focus of the unit, or when teaching genre, the focus of the unit converges with the units taught in reading workshop and writing workshop. To see how instruction and learning can be connected across workshops, see Figure 8.1.

FIGURE 8.1 Connections Between Workshops

Topics Across Workshops

Language Workshop Unit	What might be happening during reading workshop?	What might be happening during writing workshop?
Identifying themes and character development in a chapter-book-length text.	1. Identifying theme within individual reading texts. Using T-charts in response journals to propose theme ideas and provide evidence from text to back up the thinking. 2. Determining importance of details in text and the relation of these details to the story, plot, and characters. 3. Developing vocabulary to assist comprehension of text.	Personal Narrative 1. Focusing small in writing. Sticking to one meaningful idea or event. 2. Identifying author's feelings and showing feelings and ideas through details. Showing, not telling.
Book Title: *Because of Winn-Dixie*, by Kate DiCamillo	Book Titles: Multiple titles for individual reading in book bags, book boxes, and reading and literature groups for small-group instruction	Book Titles: Mentor texts identified by teacher
• Note and talk about author's craft: plot and character development. • Use comparisons and analogies to explain ideas. • Refer to knowledge gained during discussion with peers.	• Learn new words every day from reading. • Recognize when reader doesn't know what a work means and use a variety of fix-up strategies to figure it out. • Use comparisons and analogies to explain ideas.	• Create a sequence of events that unfolds naturally. • Introduce character (author) through precise details.
Student Product: • Response journal entries • Participation in discussion • Response to literature	Student Product: • Reading logs • Reading response journal entries	Student Product: • Personal narrative • Poems • Picture books
Assessment Tool: Literature response rubric	Assessment Tool: Running records Anecdotal notes Response journal rubric	Assessment Tool: Personal narrative rubric Checklist developed from mentor text for poetry and picture books (It is best to use a rubric when assessing a grade-level standard or expectation.)

Unit-of-Study Content Objectives

Units of study organized around themes relating to linguistically diverse students might include any theme or historical trend that poses an inquiry for students regarding

- defining world problems
- framing social trends and issues
- developing personal choices
- finding the big ideas or general topics in a body of work
- analyzing characters' actions in relation to the general topics
- generating statements about the author's point or message about a topic
- expressing opinions

Units of study organized around the elements of a genre can include

- narrative
  - antagonist and protagonist viewpoints
  - author's purpose
  - character
  - dialogue
  - mood
  - point of view
  - plot and setting
  - voice
  - symbols
  - memoir
- nonfiction
  - cause and effect
  - chronological order
  - comparison and contrast
  - editorial
  - interview
  - lead
  - main idea development
  - problem and solution
  - propaganda techniques
  - viewpoint
  - persuasion
- poetry
  - language
  - meaning
  - elements of poetry
  - figurative language
  - alliteration
  - onomatopoeia
  - imagery
  - mood
  - metaphor

Units of study organized around specific strategies can include

- revising meaning
- monitoring
- playing with language
- developing literary language
- generalizing
- evaluating
- determining importance
- asking questions
- making inferences
- synthesizing text, retelling
- tapping schemata, prior knowledge
- predicting
- organizing ideas
- figuring out unknown words
- visualizing
- making connections

Unit-of-Study Focus

Units focusing on similar themes, genres, or strategies can overlap from one workshop to another, but the work should begin in language workshop. It is not always possible for all three workshops to align to the same focus and goals; however, when appropriate, student learning can be accelerated and deepened by such alignment. Aligning units across more than one workshop also increases consistency and coherence across the curriculum.

Remember that the desire is for students to acquire language, develop strategy use, ponder a topic, and learn to think critically. During workshop instruction and interaction, students are focused on language comprehension. As listeners our students need to do more than listen to the conversation and understand what is being explicitly stated. Children need to draw inferences from conversation and understand implicit messages in conversation and text. They need to consider the context of a discussion or written work. By doing so, they develop a strategy for analyzing and participating in discussion (Wren 2000).

Features of Units of Study

Units of study are curriculum guides that focus your teaching for four to five weeks. The units fit together like interlocking links to develop a scope and sequence for workshop instruction. The units are fluid in order to develop maximum capacity for student interest and ability and help you focus on what you are currently teaching and what you are going to teach next according to standards and student needs. The remainder of this chapter focuses on developing an understanding of how the units fit together across workshops with a focus on language workshop, and how to write and implement these types of plans.

English Acquisition Levels and Frames for Instruction

Before planning instruction for your unit of study, consider the language levels of English learners and the language needs of the mainstream English speakers in your classroom. Figure 8.2 shows three different ways to frame your instruction for English learners. While three categories don't begin to describe the individual needs of your English learners and linguistic-minority students, the category, or frame, corresponds to classroom and student needs. A first-grade student has different educational needs from a seventh grader; however, if the seventh grader is new to the country and new to English, he may be acquiring language just as a first grader acquires English. Both students have distinct needs and are on a very different time line for acquiring English at a level that will allow them to learn grade-level content, so there are different frames of instruction to consider for each.

The first frame is *grades K–2 mixed acquisition levels*. This frame addresses a few of the needs of students acquiring language in primary classrooms. Some students are English learners, others may be linguistic-minority students, and others may be English-only students who are acquiring academic language and acquiring the discourse of formal schooling. The focus of this frame is on developing early literacy skills, language comprehension, acquisition of conversational English, and acquisition of academic language in content areas relevant to very young students.

The second frame is *grades 3–8 mixed acquisition levels*. This frame addresses the language development needs of students in middle and upper grades who are in mixed-ability classrooms. This frame focuses on domain knowledge, academic language, and specific knowledge about genres, including reading and discussing specific genres while developing the skills to write in those genres. This level is of particular importance because many students in middle and upper grades who are struggling in school were identified as English learners in kindergarten but have failed to make adequate progress. Without intense and specific instruction, these students will not have the language and content background necessary to be successful in high school and beyond.

The third frame is *grades 3–8 early acquisition levels*. This frame addresses the language development needs of students in middle and upper grades who are new to English. This can include students who are recent immigrants or newcomers to school in the United States. This frame focuses on the acquisition of English by developing listening and speaking skills. Instruction for these students also must be specific and targeted to student needs because they don't have as many years to acquire interpersonal and academic language as students who enter the educational system in kindergarten.

When planning a unit of study, choose lessons according to your students' acquisition levels. Chapters 9 and 10 list possible lessons for units of study designed around themes and strategies. These units list lessons focused on specific frames of instruction. You can pick and choose lessons depending on the frame that applies to your students.

Language Workshop Unit Planning

Units of study for language workshop can be developed around a content theme, or comprehension strategies. Each of these types of unit has specific purposes to teach, model, and guide students toward the use of language and the ability to read, write, and talk well. To begin planning a unit, it is important to recognize the components in each unit that you use to inform, teach, model, and support students. These components include

■ Language goals: Consider what language frame (as described in the previous section) you are working with. For instruction, consider the

LANGUAGE WORKSHOP

Unit of Study ——————→ Frames of Instruction

Grade	K–2 Mixed Acquisition Levels	3–8 Mixed Acquisition Levels	3–8 Early Acquisition Levels
Goals	• Develop oral communication skills in English. • Use English to interact in classroom and social settings. • Add words to familiar knowledge domains. • Add new domain knowledge from developmentally appropriate content studies. • Promote the continued development of primary language.	• Use English to construct, process and obtain content matter information orally and written. • Use appropriate and effective strategies to construct domain knowledge and academic language. • Sort and connect relationships among words in knowledge domains. • Promote the continued development of primary language. • Respond and elaborate appropriately with peers and teacher in academic and informal conversations.	• Rapidly acquire the use of English in socially and culturally appropriate ways. • Foster acquisition of functional language while developing academic knowledge in primary language. • Learn strategies to extend communication abilities.
Lesson Structures	• Simultaneously engage students in listening, speaking, reading and writing modalities. • Foster language acquisition through authentic, functional language lessons. • Model language and scaffold language structures to promote understanding. • Represent information visually.	• Simultaneously engage students in listening, speaking, reading and writing modalities. • Use oral and written academic language features in content and genre studies. • Promote oral and written response and elaboration with peers and teacher in academic discourses. • Promote the synthesis and evaluation of ideas and information. • Model language and scaffold language structures to promote understanding. • Represent information visually.	• Develop effective language use for social and cultural purposes. • Simultaneously engage students in listening, speaking, reading and writing modalities. • Foster language acquisition through authentic, functional language lessons. • Model language and scaffold language structures to promote understanding. • Represent information visually.

Before planning instruction for your unit of study, consider the language levels of English learners and the language needs of the mainstream English speakers in your classroom. Teach the types of lessons that apply to the language needs of your students. Then, pick and choose from the lessons in each unit of study (see Chapters 9 and 10) to fill in your lesson plan grid for the unit of study. The grid is a way to plot your anchor minilessons in order to give you a range for your work and an understanding of what you are accomplishing in a specified amount of time.

Resources for goals and lesson structures include: *ESL Standards for Pre-K–12 Students* (TESOL 1997), *Kidwatching* (Owocki and Goodman 2002), and *Speaking and Listening for Preschool through Third Grade* (New Standards 2001).

FIGURE 8.2 Frames of Instruction

strengths of your students and what they need to do to increase their abilities in English.

- Overall teaching focus: Consider the focus of the unit of study. Is it a genre study, a strategy study, or a thematic study? Stating your objectives keeps your unit on track and helps you assess student progress along the way.
- Minilesson choices: Consider what minilessons would be appropriate in the unit of study. You will need to plan minilessons that are explicit but focused on meaningful applications of reading, writing, and discussion.
- Books: choose books to support learning that model form, ideas, and language. Picture books, literary chapter books for children, and high-quality nonfiction books provide content information and models of language and genre. You should use materials that you love, or find exciting, so that your passion for literacy comes through with the reading of content information and mentor texts.
- Student products and assessment: Consider what work you want students to produce during the unit. Think about what students will know and be able to do during the unit. Also consider what you will assess. Your goals will probably include oral language as well as some written language including reports, language journals, dialogue journals, and responses to literature.

After mapping out these components on the language workshop planning sheet (see Figure 8.3 for a blank planning sheet; Chapters 9 and 10 have examples of fully planned units for explanation), design your unit of study by mapping out the minilessons on the block planning sheet (Figure 8.4). Figure 8.5 is a sample of the unit titled "Lessons for All Units." On the block planning sheet I write each minilesson in the appropriate square, depending on when I anticipate teaching it. If I think I will need to repeat a lesson, or go into the topic in depth, I write it down more than once. I also leave several boxes blank in order to plan some lessons after I assess student progress. These plans are fluid; if students need more help and scaffolding, then I provide it. If the students are learning more rapidly than the pace of my plans, then I adjust my plans accordingly.

Chapters 9 and 10 are designed to support your instruction. There are three theme units in Chapter 9 and several strategy lessons in Chapter 10. You can also pick and choose from the lessons in each unit of study to fill in your lesson plan grid for a unit you create. The grid is a way to plot the minilessons that anchor your unit of study. Anchor minilessons are the lessons essential to teach in any given unit (Akhavan 2004). It is important to plan your unit in order to give you a range for your work and an understanding of what you are accomplishing in a specified amount of time.

A Sample Unit for Language Workshop

Figure 8.5 is a unit that you might choose to teach at the beginning of the school year. This unit lays out the expectations for language workshop and

LANGUAGE WORKSHOP

Charts and Graphics to Aid Language Development

Title of Study _____

Lesson Choices	Teaching Focus	Books and Resources

FIGURE 8.3 Blank Unit-of-Study Planning Sheet

LANGUAGE WORKSHOP

Unit-of-Study Planning Grid

Monday	Tuesday	Wednesday	Thursday	Friday

© 2006 by Nancy Akhavan from *Help! My Kids Don't All Speak English.* Portsmouth, NH: Heinemann.

FIGURE 8.4   Block Planning Sheet

LANGUAGE WORKSHOP

Charts and Graphics to Aid Language Development	Lesson Choices	Teaching Focus	Books and Resources
Several charts should be created to show students the basics of the workshop: The daily agenda for the workshop How to partner share How to jot in the language notebook How to be a respectful listener How to be open with ideas and share ideas with the group	How to Work in the Workshop—*Showing students the materials and resources, teaching the routines* How to Partner Share—*Modeling how to talk with a partner about an idea or book* How to Talk About Your Ideas (and Not Be Embarrassed)—*Creating an accepting environment where all participants' voices are valued and students value one another* Keeping a Language Log—*Teaching how to write notes in the language notebook* Forming an Opinion (Yes, It's OK!)—*Modeling how to share ideas and opinions in respectful ways* Determining the Gist of a Nonfiction Text—*Discussing the point of various nonfiction texts and then modeling how to share the point of the text with a partner or the whole group* Asking Questions About What We Read—*Modeling the thinking and questioning process while reading*	The overall goal of this unit is to familiarize students with the routines of language workshop. This process can include any management issues that arise, such as how to move about the classroom, retrieve notebooks, and sit with a partner or small groups. Any lesson taught during this unit will introduce students to • Collaborating • Responding to books • Forming an idea or opinion from information • Understanding opposing views • Making comparisons • Reasoning through text • Making text connections • Making important outside connections • Managing materials • Speaking during group and partner shares	Any book that matches the lesson objective, is appealing to the children, and is enjoyable and useful to the teacher. (See Appendix B for lists of suggested books.)

© 2006 by Nancy Akhavan from *Help! My Kids Don't All Speak English*. Portsmouth, NH: Heinemann.

FIGURE 8.5 Planning Sheet: Lessons for All Units

helps the students work as a community of learners. This unit prepares students for the work to be done and develops skills so that they can independently participate in discussion, jot in notebooks, lead an inquiry, listen, or pose questions. The essential learning goals for this unit relate to the understanding students should develop about how to communicate in the workshop and why participating as a member of the group is important for individual and group learning. The minilesson teaches specific skills and objectives related to these essential learning goals.

Scope of Work for Several Grade Levels

So far I have discussed planning for language workshop over several weeks as developed in a unit of study. The sample unit titled Lessons for All Units is composed of essential learning objectives that are building blocks for other units. In addition to focusing on the individual units of study, it is important to organize learning over the school year so that learning is aligned to standards and grade-level goals and so that learning remains coherent and valuable. It is also important to envision how learning expands over multiple grade levels. Figure 8.6 is a sample curriculum map that lays out expectations for language workshop over several grade levels. Each section lists what students should know and be able to do at each grade level. This list is not inclusive of all skills and strategies, or essential learning goals, that a student must have; it focuses on language ability and the ability to analyze and discuss ideas related to topics and themes.

Figure 8.6 organizes the information by grade level so the development of a continuous program is easy to track. You can see the progress an English learner might make from kindergarten to eighth grade. These language goals are based on national standards developed by the National Center on Education and the Economy and the standards for English learners developed by Teachers of English to Speakers of Other Languages. This curriculum map is only a suggestion for expected benchmarks. What is most important is that you develop a curriculum plan that dovetails into other grade levels so that you and your colleagues are collaborating across grade levels to meet student needs.

LANGUAGE WORKSHOP

Scope of Workshop Focus

Kindergarten	First Grade	Second Grade	Third Grade
• Tell what they liked about a story and why	• Make text-to-self, text-to-text, and text-to-world connections	• Make text-to-self, text-to-text, and text-to-world connections beyond superficial levels	• Participate in group discussion
• Draw a picture in response to a story	• Refer explicitly to parts of the text when presenting or defending their connections	• Recognize and talk about organizing structures within genres	• Ask for clarification from the speaker
• Recognize and discuss story elements: character, setting, plot	• Begin to make text-to-text connections between books by same author	• Infer cause and effect	• Build on a conversation by extending another's contribution
• Retell character, problem, solution	• Politely disagree when appropriate	• Discuss themes in one book and reoccurring themes across works	• Ask other students questions, requiring them to support claims or arguments
• Listen carefully to each other	• Make predictions about what might happen next	• Do author studies	• Indicate when their own or others' ideas need further backup
• Learn to make text-to-self connections by using their own experiences to make sense of text	• Talk about motives of characters or people in real events	• Participate in a group discussion	• Discuss underlying themes or messages
• State their ideas on character feelings and provide proof from the text (either words or pictures): "Maria is sad." "Where in the book did it tell you that?"	• Describe cause and effect of events	• Politely challenge one another	• Identify and discuss themes across works
	• Write simple evaluative statements about text: "I like the story because . . ."; "I like the part when . . ."	• Build on conversations	• Examine reasons for characters' actions, accounting narrative for situations and motives
	• Recognize differences between fiction and nonfiction	• Make comments with reference to text	• Relay connections to real-life experiences beyond superficial info
	• Describe new information they have learned	• Determine what characters are like from what they say or do and from how the author portrays them	• Use structure of informational text to retrieve info
		• Recognize and discuss story elements—setting character, and events—in detail	• Describe and synthesize this info into new thinking
		• Write an evaluative statement identifying the big idea or theme	• Recognize and talk about organizing structures within genres
		• Write a story map including setting, character, problem, solution, and overall theme	• Do an author study (minimum of one author)
		• Write text connections stating a specific part of the text or quotes	• Identify and discuss at least two story elements independently—content, point of view, plot, beginnings, endings, character development
		• Write a letter to an author (in conjunction to an author study) telling him or her what they think and why or asking questions	• Begin response journals, jot notes
		• Identify conventions in their nonfiction text	• Support interpretation, theme, or text-to-self connections by making specific references to the text
		• Discuss how, why, and what if questions	• Write wonderings and connections that are supported by evidence in the text
		• Follow the story line and relate later parts of story to earlier parts of book in terms of themes and cause and effect	• Write how their evaluation of the theme or big idea changed their views and understandings—new thinking
			• Explain figurative language: metaphor, simile; discuss author's word choice
			• Discuss plot and setting with specific events, focusing on cause and effect
			• Analyze and interpret events through cause and effect in historical nonfiction text
			• Describe in their own words what new info they have learned from nonfiction text and how it relates to their prior knowledge
			• Identify and discuss theme or message of text

© 2006 by Nancy Akhavan from *Help! My Kids Don't All Speak English*. Portsmouth, NH: Heinemann.

FIGURE 8.6 Scope of Essential Learning Goals (*Grades 4–8 on pages 96–97*.)

Scope of Workshop Focus

LANGUAGE WORKSHOP

Fourth Through Eighth Grade	Focus for Grades 4–8 as Students Progress

Understand Text Structures and Conventions in Literature, Literary Nonfiction, and Nonfiction Multimedia Print

- Consider the function of point of view
- Consider how point of view impacts the story or issue
- Identify the different types of point of view
- Recount interesting events

Character Development

- Examine character action
- Understand and evaluate character motivation
- Identify character monologue, dialogue, and appearance

Discuss Theme or Issue

- Identify theme throughout novel
- Demonstrate how the author uses character to help reader infer theme
- Use inference to explain what is happening in a text or issue
- Draw conclusions about character, event, context, and setting
- Begin self-selection of text
- Synthesize, analyze, and evaluate information

Speaking and Listening

- Participate in group discussions
- Actively solicit other's comments and opinions
- Volunteer contributions and respond when solicited by others in group
- Give reasons in support of opinions they express
- Clarify or expand on comments
- Defend and elaborate on position or statement using specific examples from the text
- Listen intently to fellow students and add to or question the previous comments shared
- Take two issues and compare their themes
- Follow a theme throughout a piece of literature, nonfiction text, or issue from the Internet or television and make and support statements about that theme
- Share and request information in conversations
- Express ideas, feelings, and needs
- Indicate interests, opinions, and preferences in group work
- Negotiate solutions to problems and interpersonal misunderstandings
- Engage listeners' attention verbally and nonverbally
- Respond to group "small talk"
- Listen to and incorporate a peer's feedback into analysis

Students are adept at all tasks but language development continues.

- Use a more sophisticated level of conversation
- Volunteer opinions and reasoning without constant solicitation from teacher
- Write more developed notes
- Establish independent group work and begin running discussions with minimal topic suggestion(s) by teachers
- Actively and effectively participate in both speaking and listening aspects of individual group meetings
- Begin to select texts that are appropriate to their level (independent)
- Use persona and a context for writing (strong voice throughout)
- Express and support an opinion by using references to the text
- Connect prior knowledge about subject or topic to elaborate and/or develop an opinion
- Demonstrate understanding of grade-level-appropriate literary work
- Provide closure or reflection when writing or responding to group work
- Reflect at length
- Locate appropriate information in text or reference materials

© 2006 by Nancy Akhavan from *Help! My Kids Don't All Speak English.* Portsmouth, NH: Heinemann.

FIGURE 8.6 *(Continued)*

Responding to Literature

- Express an opinion (and support it with knowledge and facts from text)
- Take a stance on one of the story elements: character, conflict, setting
- Demonstrate understanding of literary work—theme, message (how the author uses characters, events, conflict to show this)
- Provide closure, reflection (summary of thoughts)
- Restate or summarize information
- Read info, internalize, and discuss it, and write it in own words
- Relate new information to prior knowledge, experience, and related topics
- Write a detailed explanation combining what they knew with new info they have gained
- Extend and explain ideas and actions
- Take the topic and say more about it
- Introduce the ideas of taking an initial inquiry and then extending it

Vocabulary and Language

- Practice new language
- Use context to construct meaning
- Use language chunks to try increasingly more sophisticated language features
- Ask for clarification of unknown words
- Keep notes for language learning

FIGURE 8.6

CHAPTER NINE

Content-Based Language Lessons

Content Study: Immigration

1.1 What Is Immigration?

Content Objective: Develop background knowledge about immigration.

Language Objective: Self-monitoring and self-evaluating understanding of conversation and text. Associate information from diagrams or charts with information from class discussion to learn vocabulary.

Response: Class discussion and whole-group chart listing known facts about immigration.

Time Line: This lesson can be repeated over two to three days until the class has explored all materials available.

1. Purpose of the Minilesson

One culturally relevant theme to explore with children of diverse backgrounds is immigration (see Figure 9.1). Through the years, I have worked with students from numerous countries who each had their own family story to share. I have also worked with blended families who had multiple heritages or perspectives to share. Students need to have an understanding of what immigration is and how immigration has affected the lives of people in the United States. The lesson focuses on building background knowledge.

This lesson includes activities in which students reflect on their knowledge and then explore materials to add to their information base. Introduce this lesson by connecting students to the task: "Today we are going to explore a new topic that affects everyone in our class in some way. The topic is immigration; some of you are recent immigrants, while others of you had family that immigrated to the United States many years ago. Some of you may know

LANGUAGE WORKSHOP

Content Study: Immigration

Charts and Graphics to Aid Language Development	Lesson Choices	Teaching Focus	Books and Resources
Concept map	What Is Immigration?	Develop background knowledge about immigration.	Bierman, Carol. 1998. *Journey to Ellis Island: How My Father Came to America.*
"What Is Immigration?" chart	How Immigration Affects People's Lives	Describe and explain how the lure of a better life influenced the movement of people to the United States, examine the central issues and problems from the past, describing why people in the past chose to immigrate here.	Bunting, Eve. 1990. *How Many Days to America? A Thanksgiving Story.*
"What the Parents Want/What the Children Want" chart	Reasons People Leave Their Countries ("Push/Pull" chart)		Bunting, Eve. 1999. *A Picnic in October.*
"Push/Pull" T-chart	Immigrant Bundles		Ellis Island Oral History Project. 1997. *I Was Dreaming to Come to America.*
	What Happened at Ellis Island?	Identify factors that push people from their countries and factors that pull them to new countries.	Freedman, Russel. 1995. *Immigrant Kids.*
	Sharing Your Family History		Hest, Amy. 1997. *When Jessie Came Across the Sea.*
	Look Around—We Are All Different	Describe different outcomes for immigrants at Ellis Island.	Hoobler, Dorothy, and Thomas Hoobler. 2003. *We Are All Americans: Voices of the Immigrant Experience.*
	Immigration and the World	Develop understanding and sensitivity to the plight of immigrants.	Levine, Ellen. 1994. *If Your Name Was Changed at Ellis Island.*
	Interviewing People About Their History	Recognize differences between class members. Students share information like their favorite foods, their hopes and dreams, their education plans. Then students relate these opportunities to life in the United States.	Maestro, Betsy. 1996. *Coming to America: The Story of Immigration.*
	Writing an Informational Report	Use English to obtain, process, construct, and provide subject matter information in written form.	Norris, Betsy, and Donna Brock. 2003. *Immigration (Primary Sources Teaching Kit, Grades 4–8).*
			Shea, Pegi Deitz. 1996. *The Whispering Cloth: A Refugee's Story.*
			Tarbescu, Edith. 1998. *Annushka's Voyage.*
			Woodruff, Elvira. 1999. *The Memory Coat.*
			Kids Discover. 2002. "Ellis Island." 12 (5).
			Kids Discover. 2000. "Immigration."
			Life: The American Immigrant Issue. 2004. 20 September.
			Smithsonian. 2004. "American Odyssey." September.

FIGURE 9.1 Unit-of-Study Design Sheet: Immigration

your family history, but some of you may know only the history of other family members. We are going to learn more about ourselves or other family members. We are going to gather information from our own knowledge and several books I have available and add this information to our chart."

2. Instruction Point: Gather and Share Information
Have an easel and chart pad near the class gathering area. Focus student attention on a chart with the following topics listed:

- What is immigration?
- Who is an immigrant?
- Where do immigrants move?
- Why do immigrants move?
- How do they start new lives?

Next I would discuss each question and record the information students offer. Explain that they are going to do research to get more information to add to the chart. Then break the students into five groups and assign each group one question for further investigation. Have students write their focus question on a sticky note. (It works best to have students use clipboards on their laps. Then they can add to their notes and see their focus question at the same time.) Then set out five tubs filled with books and other resources on immigration (for suggested books see Appendix B). Students peruse the materials with their group and tab pages that provide information for their focus question. They can gather information from text, pictures, diagrams, or stories.

3. Engagement
Students share the information they gathered with the whole class. Encourage students to explain their thinking while referring to the page, picture, or diagram with the important information.

4. Closure
Review work of the day; recap the concept of immigration.

1.2 How Immigration Affects People's Lives

> **Content Objective:** Describe and explain how the lure of a better life influenced the movement of people to the United States, and examine the central issues and problems from the past, describing why people in the past chose to immigrate here.
>
> **Language Objective:** Clarify and restate information as needed.
>
> **Response:** Whole-class chart and notes in language notebooks.

1. Introduce the Purpose of the Minilesson
Gather students in the class meeting area and tell them of your goals and aspirations for something special in your life (perhaps share about how you

dreamed of college, or tell of a future dream, like wanting to go to back-packing or on a special trip). Explain to students that for many years people have dreamed of coming to America and their dreams have led them to this country. Not only did immigration change their lives, but it changed the background of the people living in the United States and gave depth and meaning to many people's lives.

2. Instruction Point: Read an Excerpt from a Touchstone Text and Model Thinking

Read a section from *Marianthe's Story*, by Aliki (1998). Discuss with students how Marianthe feels in school. Write these ideas down on a chart in the meeting area. Specifically identify words in the passage that help you inter-pret Marianthe's feelings. This step is when *you* model for the students what they are going to do during the read-aloud time. You read a snippet of text, and then you tell them your thinking. Make your thinking transpar-ent. One useful excerpt is on page 4.

Read: "The people in our village were so close; they shared the good and the bad like a family. During the war, they mourned together when so many people were killed."

Share: "I think that the people in the village were devastated by the war. The picture on this page makes me think that the woman and man are beside themselves because someone they love is dead. Perhaps this is why a family might choose to leave their country and immigrate to another one. I cannot imagine how horrible it is to lose someone you love to war."

3. Engage Students in Responding to the Touchstone Text Model

Have students talk about their thoughts in pairs for about one minute. Re-mind them to share what they think the family in *Marianthe's Story* might feel and want to change. After they talk, have a couple of students share their ideas. Invite students to think deeply about the family's desires and decision during the read-aloud.

The first three steps are the minilesson, which leads into the read-aloud for the day's workshop.

4. Encourage Students to Speak About Their Ideas During the Read-Aloud

Begin reading *Marianthe's Story* from the beginning. Read a few pages at a time and pause for students to talk with their partners about the thoughts and feelings of the characters in the book. Encourage students to think about how the characters felt and why they chose to leave their country. Take notes of student thinking on a chart with the headings "What the Par-ents Want" and "What the Children Want." Encourage students in grades 3 through 8 to write notes in their language response notebooks.

This lesson can be repeated on several days with different picture books. Encourage students to ask peers for their opinions and ideas. Re-mind them to engage with their partners and listen attentively. Encourage them to think about their own dreams and the dreams, or histories, of their families and draw parallels to the plight of the families in the texts you choose.

1.3 Reasons People Leave Their Countries

Content Objective: Identify factors that push people from their countries and factors that pull them to new countries.

Language Objective: Negotiate disputes with peers over interpretation of facts, negotiate meaning, respond appropriately to teacher and peer prompting, and discuss information from a text.

Response: Class-generated T-chart labled "Push/Pull."

1. Introduce the Purpose of the Minilesson

Sandra DeCarli, a fifth-grade teacher at Manchester G.A.T.E. Elementary School in Fresno, California, creates a "Push/Pull" chart with her students in order to understand reasons people immigrate. She wants her students to understand multiple perspectives, so she has students explore what factors *push* people from their countries and what factors *pull* people to a new country. Sandra doesn't have many English learners in her room, but she does have many students from linguistically diverse backgrounds. Many of their families speak a language other than English at home. So Sandra spends time building knowledge and vocabulary related to immigration. Before the lesson in which the class creates the chart together (with Sandra acting as scribe), she has her students research push and pull factors in multiple resources on immigration in her room. Students can keep their research organized by writing notes on index cards, sticky notes, or in their language response notebooks. Sandra gets her students to focus on what makes people leave their countries and what attracts them to the United States.

2. Focus Students on Similarities Between People

Sandra begins the lesson by having students "look around" themselves, by examining the classroom and school and listing the diverse groups that attend the school. She wants her students to see that the school is diverse, and not everyone is the same. She then encourages them to think about the history of immigration in the United States and to realize that different people had different reasons for leaving their countries and coming to America.

The chart that she created with her class is shown in Figure 9.2.

1.4 Immigrant Bundles

Content Objective: Develop an understanding of the difficulties of leaving home by describing the amount of personal items an immigrant

FIGURE 9.2 "Push/Pull" Chart

Push	Pull
• War	• Opportunity to work
• Unfair treatment	• Freedom—religious and equal rights
• Tyrannical leadership	• Job choices
• Lack of food/famine	• Voting
• Drought	• Fertile land for agriculture
• Low or no wages	• Land availability
• Slavery (left by force)	• Democratic form of government
• Dangerous environment	• Riches, wealth
	• Education
	• Join other family members

typically brings with him to the United States. Develop understanding of personal belongings and personal wealth in relation to monetary items and nonmonetary items.

Activity: Design a bundle of items that an immigrant family might take on their journey to a new home. Use information gathered from cultures and needs of new immigrants to decide what items to choose for the bundle.

Response: Poster depicting the items chosen by an immigrant family for their journey.

1. Introduce the Purpose of the Minilesson

This lesson is also from Sandra DeCarli's classroom. After her class researches and explores topics and information on immigration, she asks her students to portray the information they have synthesized on a poster depicting a trunk, or bundle, of items a person would pack when leaving her country. She encourages students to choose an immigrant background that appeals to them or that reflects their own heritage.

Her guidelines include the following directions: "Draw something to remind the immigrants of their homeland and something to remind them of their family. Include something they will use in their new country and something to entertain them during their voyage, or travel." Remember that the focus of the activity is for students to understand the difference between what we have in our homes and how little an immigrant might bring with him on his journey. A good example of how much an immigrant brings on a journey to the United States is in *Esperanza Rising* (Ryan 2002). This is a beautiful story of a young girl who emigrates from Mexico under duress.

1.5 What Happened at Ellis Island?

Content Objective: Design a concept map describing different outcomes for immigrants at Ellis Island.

Language Objective: In small groups, discuss the feelings, needs, and goals of people in different situations. Ask for clarification to interpret and understand discussion.

This lesson revolves around the students discussing the goals and desires of the immigrants, the employees at Ellis Island, and the families waiting for their loved ones to arrive. Students will write notes under the appropriate column heading on a concept map (see Appendix A) and use vocabulary related to the process at Ellis Island.

Response: Group concept map, individual concept map, and whole-group discussion.

1. Show Concept Map
The map will list broad categories: employees at Ellis Island, incoming immigrants, and families waiting for loved ones to arrive. Discuss how the class will look for clues to how these people felt and thought from several books and text resources in the room.

2. Instruction Point: Read Aloud a Sample Text
Choose an example from one text for each area on the concept map and discuss your thinking. First, read the section of text; then tell your thinking. Make your thinking transparent, and add it to the chart. Model this at least twice. Tell students how make notes about their thinking on their own concept map (it works best when students work in pairs and share one map).

3. Engagement
Ask them to talk with their partners quickly about the goal for today's workshop and what they are going to do together.

4. Invite Small-Group Inquiry
Break the class into pairs to study the resources you've made available to find evidence of how people felt and what they thought while being at Ellis Island. Each pair should have at least one text to read and look through. Students take notes on their shared map.

5. Return to Meeting Area for Whole-Class Share
Elicit information, observations, and ideas from the class and create a chart. The chart is a large concept map. Include what the students think and the resources where they found the information.

1.6 Sharing Your Family History

Language Objective: (Adapted from *TESOL Standards* 1997, 87.)

Goal 2: Use English to achieve academically in all content areas.

FIGURE 9.3 Catherine's Family History Report

My Family's Immigrant History
Catherine Chooljian

I am an immigrant of mainly Armenian descent. I am half Armenian, one-quarter German, and one-quarter English and Irish. My father's family was originally from Armenia. My mother's parents were descended from both German immigrants and people who lived in America during the Revolutionary War. One even helped write the Constitution of the United States!

My grandfather on my father's side was the second son of Haroutiun Chooljian, who immigrated to the United States in the early 1900's. He came to escape the growing persecution in Armenia, and traveled by boat to Ellis Island. He married another Armenian, Arax, and moved to California. They started a vineyard near Del Rey, California, by staking claim to a forty acre plot of land. Haroutiun was allowed to walk around as much land as he wanted to claim, and place his marker. I wish it was that easy to purchase land today!

My grandparents on my father's side did not have as easy a time getting to the United States. My great-grandmother, Agnes, had to pretend to be dead on a pile of corpses to escape being killed herself. She and her sister, who also pretended to be dead, used the underground to escape the Armenian genocide. My great-grandfather, Dikran Booroojian, came across the ocean on a ship with his family before the genocide began, but they came because his father had been killed. They lived in New York until their son joined the Navy in World War II. He was stationed in San Francisco, and when they came to see him they liked California so much they stayed here.

My family is so fascinating I could write a million pages and not run out of things to say about them! My ancestors grew up in distant places, and all of them seem to have had a sad or terrible experience. My Mother and Father have amazing parents, grandparents, and great-grandparents. Someday, I hope to find out more!

Standard 2: Use English to obtain, process, construct, and provide subject matter information in written form. Student will locate reference material and write a family history paper. The student will revise in order to improve the narrative.

Response: Student will write a narrative account on family history including details about when the family settled in the city where they live and when the family immigrated to the United States.

1. Introduce the Purpose of the Minilesson
Sandra finishes her immigration unit by having the students write their family histories. She gives the criteria she expects to be in the paper when she explains the assignment and helps each student gather details to put in her paper. She teaches the students how to interview family members for more information and she models for students how an engaging family history is written. Figure 9.3 shows an example from a student in Sandra's classroom. The family history project helps students understand who they are and the hardship that their families have faced. They also develop value for the diverse backgrounds represented in their classrooms.

Other lessons in this unit might include

- Look Around—We Are All Different
  Objective: Recognize differences between class members. Students share information like their favorite foods, their hopes and dreams, and education plans. Then students relate these dreams to life in the United States.
- Immigration and the World
  Objective: Students develop an understanding of the movement patterns of ethnic groups in America. They consider trends and facts to decide where people move and why.
- Interviewing People About Their History
  Objective: Students develop an understanding of and sensitivity to the plight of immigrants by interviewing people who have immigrated in the United States.
- Writing an Informational Report: Immigration and the United States or Immigration and Change
  Objective: Students write an informational report focusing on two or three facts they find important about immigration. This would be most appropriate for students in teaching frames two and three. The report would include organizing structures of nonfiction pieces like a lead, headings, and description.

Content Study: Peace and Tolerance

2.1 How Do You Imagine Peace? (See Figure 9.4)

Content Objective: Consider a topic from multiple perspectives and state ideas about the concept of peace.

Language Objective: Students build abilities to discuss information from books:

- Cite important details from text
- Refer to knowledge gained in the discussion
- Restate their own ideas clearly when the listeners don't understand
- Use comparisons and analogies to explain ideas (New Standards 2001, 220)

Response: Class-generated semantic map and class-generated cubing organizer.

Overview

The first lesson of any content study sets up the topic to be examined during the next several weeks. This unit of study revolves around a process called *cubing*. Cubing is an inquiry process where the class considers a topic, or concept, from six viewpoints. It is called cubing because, like cubes, the procedure has six dimensions for critical thinking. The cubing process begins with the first lesson and takes many lessons to complete. For

LANGUAGE WORKSHOP

Content Study: Peace and Tolerance

Charts and Graphics to Aid Language Development	Lesson Choices	Teaching Focus	Books and Resources
Semantic map	How Do You Imagine Peace?	Consider a topic from multiple perspectives and state ideas about the concept of peace.	Bakuill, Jane. 2003. *If Peace Is . . .*
Cubing diagram	The Colors of Peace and Tolerance	Students build abilities to discuss information from books.	Garrison, Jennifer. 2001. *A Million Visions of Peace.*
"Item/Occurrence/Association" T-chart	Peace Begins with Tolerance	Express feelings and ideas, participate in conversation, use context to construct meaning.	Heard, Georgia. 2002. *This Place I Know: Poems of Comfort.*
"Character Actions" chart	Appreciating Someone Who Thinks Differently Than You Do	Relate feelings of calm, happiness, fright, anger, and so on to colors and objects in order to visualize emotions.	Henkes, Kevin. 1996. *Chrysanthemum.*
"Yes/No" fact chart	Do We Have Peace in Our City, Country, and World?	Make associations between things, events, ideas, and feelings.	Hoose, Philip M. 1998. *Hey, Little Ant.*
	Do Peaceful Countries Go to War?	Analyze people's actions in relation to tolerance.	Jenkins, Emily. 2004. *My Favorite Thing (According to Alberta).*
	Interpreting Truth in Texts	Request and provide clarification and elaborate on others' ideas.	Munson, Derek. 2000. *Enemy Pie.*
	Identifying Fact and Opinion	Listen to a peer's feedback and incorporate the feedback into a written response.	Parr, Todd. 2004. *The Peace Book.*
	Reading for Fact, Writing for Emphasis	Discuss how to foster peace in the classroom and other situations.	Radinsky, Vladimir. 2003. *What Does Peace Feel Like?*
			Rylant, Cynthia. 1988. *Every Living Thing.*
			Scholes, Katharine. 1994. *Peace Begins with You.*
			Thomas, Shelley Moore. 1998. *Somewhere Today: A Book of Peace.*
			Wood, Douglas. 1999. *Grandad's Prayers of the Earth.*
			Wood, Douglas. 2001. *Old Turtle.*
			Wood, Douglas. 2003. *Old Turtle and the Broken Truth.*

© 2006 by Nancy Akhavan from *Help! My Kids Don't All Speak English.* Portsmouth, NH: Heinemann.

FIGURE 9.4   Unit-of-Study Design Sheet: Peace and Tolerance

this study, the cubing inquiry begins on the first day and is completed at the end of the unit with the assessment. The ongoing assessment in this unit is the cubing diagram students create to organize their thinking while working on their own or with a partner. In this graphic they represent their thinking in the six dimensions of the topic. (See Appendix A for the graphic organizer.)

The final assessment for this unit of study for teaching frame two is for each student to write his position on a paper separate from the graphic organizer and include facts to support his opinion (see dimension six in the following list). A final assessment for teaching frame 3 is for each student to design a poster listing the information in her graphic organizer with words, diagrams, and pictures. It is important to know your final assessment before beginning your unit of study so you will know where you are heading and what you expect students to know at the end of this three-week study.

The six dimensions in a cubing process are

1. Describe the topic.
2. Compare the topic to something else and explain why the topic makes you think of this other thing.
3. Associate the topic with something else and explain why the topic makes you think of this other thing.
4. Analyze the topic and tell what it is composed of.
5. Apply the topic and tell how it can be used or what can be done with it.
6. Argue for or against the topic. Take a position on the topic and list your opinion and the reasons to support it. (Tompkins 1997, 417)

1. Introduce the Purpose of the Minilesson
Gather students in the class meeting area, where you should have the cubing graphic organizer copied onto large paper and have several books related to peace on display. "Today we are going to begin a unit of study about peace. *Peace* can mean many different things to many different people, but the most important thing in this study is what it means to us and to our classroom community. I want you to think for a minute and then share with me what peace means to you. I want you to share your thinking with the class." Pause and let a quiet moment float.

2. Instruction Point: Invite Students to Think Aloud and Share
"Now, tell me what you are thinking." Record students' answers on a blank piece of large paper. Write "peace" in the middle of the paper and add ideas in a weblike diagram around the word. By categorizing information in this way, you create a semantic map to organize the student responses. Cluster information with similar properties together. (See Appendix A for two examples of semantic maps.) After the brainstorming, elicit three to four broad statements to write in the first column of the cubing graphic organizer.

Here are some possible student responses to the brainstorm:

Peace is . . .

- opposite of war
- calm
- when I don't fight with my brother
- when the world gets along
- happiness
- a good feeling, like when things are calm
- when people don't fight on the playground

Add a few thoughts of your own, such as

- a safe feeling I have at home
- what I wish the most for the world
- what I create within myself
- what I work toward in our classroom community

3. Engage Students in Responding to a Read-Aloud

"To further our thinking, I am going to read aloud a story about peace. The first time I read the book, I just want you to think about the story and the beauty of the words. You may feel affected by the author's message or the illustrations. Think about all of these things while I read the first time. Then we are going to read it a second time, and during the second reading we will talk about what you are thinking."

Here are some recommended texts for the read-aloud:

- *The Peace Book*, by Todd Parr (2004)—for young students and students new to English
- *Peace Begins with You*, by Katherine Scholes (1994)—for students in third through eighth grade
- *What a Wonderful World* (book and song), by George David Weiss (1995)—great for all students

4. Encourage Students to Speak About Their Ideas During and After the Read-Aloud

After the first reading, elicit responses and add them to the brainstorming sheet. Read the book and stop in places that you find moving or that students want to respond to. After the second reading, ask everyone to turn to a partner. "Now that we have had time to enjoy the beauty of this book, and think about it together, I want you to talk with your partner about what peace is. Before you begin talking, look at all the things we wrote on our clustering map. Think about what other people in the class have said, think about what affected you most in the book, think of what you know about peace from our world, and then share those ideas with your partner. Go ahead and talk."

Give the students enough time to share the first ideas that snap into their heads and then to deepen their ideas to the next level of thinking. Most often we need time to go beyond the quick list that pops into our heads when asked to share; deeper, more abstract thinking usually surfaces once the quick list has been exhausted between the partners. Move around the room and encourage students to keep discussing their ideas.

5. Invite Students to Create Statements About Peace
"Now that you have had time to share your ideas with your partners, I want everyone to gather around the easel so that we can write down our thinking. This is called a cubing organizer because like a cube, it has six dimensions. We are going to think of *peace* in six different ways during the next few weeks. Today, let's define *peace*. This is the first dimension on our chart." Elicit statements from students and fill in the chart. To ensure that the lesson goes well, gather near you two partner groups to call on. Choose partners who did well with the partner share and can tell the whole class their thinking if this part of the lesson drags.

2.2 The Colors of Peace and Tolerance
This lesson is especially designed for students new to English.

Content Objective: Students who are new to English relate feelings of calm, happiness, fright, anger, and so on to colors and objects in order to relate emotions to tangible objects and help them explain a concept (peace) in a concrete way (color).

Language Objective: Express feelings and ideas, participate in conversation, and use context to construct meaning (*TESOL Standards* 1997).

1. Read-Aloud
Read *If Kisses Were Colors*, by Janet Lawler (2003). Tell students they are going to list the feelings as you read the book. Explain that the kisses in the book are the way the mother tells her child how much she loves him.

2. Instruction Point: Reread the Text to Elicit Discussion
During the second read, plan to stop reading the book in significant places that will trigger the students to think about colors, objects, and feelings. For example, the first page of the book reads, "If kisses were pebbles, your beach would be lined with stones by the millions, of all shapes and kinds." So on the chart paper, draw a few pebbles and then write "many" or "a lot" next to the picture of pebbles. Do the same for the other objects listed in the book—draw a picture and then write key words to explain the metaphor.

3. Draw
Have each student draw a picture of peace with a partner. For example, students might draw a picture of a rose, or a bird, or a cloud. It could be anything that makes the students feel peaceful or reminds them of peace in

the world. Have students work in pairs; they should share one piece of paper between them. These diagrams should be quick draws since the focus is on the language development, not on coloring.

4. Whole-Class Share

Have students label the pictures and share with the class what they drew and why. Add these diagrams to the cubing graphic organizer under the heading "Compare."

2.3 Differences and Equality

Content Objective: Make associations between things, events, ideas, and feelings. This is the third step in the cubing diagram. The term *associate* refers to the process through which students connect one thing to another in their minds. Focus students on making associations for *peace* or *equality*.

Language Objective: Students build abilities to discuss information from books:

- Selecting, connecting, and explaining information
- Understanding and producing technical vocabulary according to a content area
- Locating information appropriate to an assignment in a text or multimedia source (*TESOL Standards* 1997, 81)

  Response: T-chart listing an idea, occurrence, or emotion and the associated object or idea.

1. Explain Associations

Begin the lesson by explaining that Eve Bunting, in her book *So Far from the Sea* (1998), associated places and things with a man's memory of an internment camp. Make a short list on a chart or whiteboard giving examples of associations from the book: a visit to the camp (event) is associated with remembered events that changed lives; being nervous (event in the book) is associated with the feelings the abandoned camp elicits in the characters; and so on. Discuss with the class other associations we have with events or things in our lives, for example, a menorah, a Christmas tree, a graduation tassel, or a bride's bouquet. Tell the class that we make associations every day in our lives to help us remember things, make sense of things, and understand. Good readers make associations in order to remember ideas and information, and in the book, Eve Bunting wrote many associations into the story to help the reader understand the impact of this moment in time on the characters.

Show the pictures in the book and explain why the Japanese Americans were placed in an internment camp. On a chart, write "What does it mean to be different?" and "What does it mean to be the equal?" Tell the students Eve Bunting shows us how this family felt they were different because of how they were treated, and now, they return to a camp that is abandoned to remember their family members and what happened to them there. Add notes to the chart as needed from the discussion and then read the book.

2. Instruction Point: Facilitate Discussion About the Book
Elicit discussion from the students about what the author is saying and what they think about what happened in the camp. Read the following quote from page 14: "It wasn't fair . . . That was mean, too. There was a lot of anger then. A lot of fear." Discuss with students what this means and add it to the chart begun in step one of the lesson.

3. Look for Associations
Ask students to think about what Eve Bunting was associating with the camp, the visit, the headstone, and the Cub Scout cloth. List these on a T-chart. Encourage the students to identify items and state their associations. Younger students or students new to English can work with you to create a class chart; older students can create the T-chart in their language response notebooks.

Item/Occurrence	Association
Visit to camp	A way of saying good-bye
Memorial (tomb, camp)	Peace, sadness

4. Share
Have students share their T-charts. Make sure they explain what the associations are between the item, emotion, or event and the object listed under "association" on their charts.

2.4 Peace Begins with Tolerance

Content Objective: Analyze character actions in relation to tolerance. Describe which characters displayed acceptance and tolerance and which characters did not.

Language Objective: Request and provide clarification, elaborate on others' ideas, listen to a peer's feedback, and incorporate the feedback into a written response (*TESOL Standards* 1997). Develop skills to understand meaning in texts and make explicit references to parts in a text when presenting their ideas.

Response: Participation in class discussion and participation in small-group share. Write a response stating why they think the characters displayed or didn't display tolerance.

1. Minilesson
Connection: "We have been discussions the six dimensions of peace. One dimension we are going to explore is analyzing how peace is around us every day in our lives. Peace is something you can't see, but you can feel it. I know that sometimes when you have a problem in class, or on the play-

ground with some else, you probably feel uncomfortable; that isn't a peaceful feeling. Peace is what we feel when things are going smoothly, when we don't feel threatened, or when everyone in class gets along."

Direct Instruction: "Good readers analyze the actions of characters while they read. Today we are going to analyze the character actions in a book and see how the characters resolved their problems. I am going to keep track of our ideas on a chart while we read and discuss the book for today."

For elementary students, *Chrysanthemum*, by Kevin Henkes (1996a), is an excellent choice for this lesson. Choices for young students and students first developing English also include *Odd Velvet*, by Mary E. Whitcomb (1998), and *The Recess Queen*, by Alexis O'Neill (2002). For students in grades 6 through 8, an alternative text is *Enemy Pie*, by Derek Munson (2000). This lesson sequence is shown with *Chrysanthemum*, but the other books work just as well.

Say, "Look at how I have organized our chart." On the top of the chart, write "Characters' Actions Show How They Feel About Others." "It is important for us to realize that peace comes from people, and we have to work to create it, so our actions tell others what we feel or think about them, and in turn we can create distrustful or peaceful situations. Now, has anyone ever had an experience in which you didn't feel good about the outcome or didn't feel peaceful?" Let students share and point to the chart and explain how you could write a note on the chart to remind you of each student's experience. "We are going to brainstorm notes together today about the character actions in the book that make others uncomfortable or show that they don't respect others."

Engagement: Have students talk with a partner about a time they remember when another person made them feel uncomfortable; then have them share how the situation was resolved.

Closure: "OK, everyone, we are ready to read. While I read *Chrysanthemum*, I want you to think about the character actions, what the characters are doing, and how it makes the other characters feel. Think about how the characters are showing or not showing tolerance for someone who is different than they are."

2. Instruction Point: Read and Facilitate Discussion

While reading, stop at points in the book that you feel will elicit discussion from your students. Talk about the character actions and then jot those actions and the results of the actions on the chart. When eliciting discussion, focus on having all students participate in the talk. If there are students who are reluctant to talk to the whole group, break them into smaller groups (three to four) and then have the small groups report out their ideas and write those ideas on the chart.

3. Assist Students in Creating a Whole-Group Response

After you finish reading the book and writing down all the ideas on the chart, assist the class in making a final statement regarding the characters in the book and tolerance. This is the moment to help them synthesize their ideas about tolerance and people's actions. You can add their final ideas to the chart as a synthesis of ideas or write them on a sentence strip or additional piece of paper and attach it to the chart. It is important that you only facilitate this process and that the students talk about their ideas and together come up with a final thought or multiple thoughts. The process is what is important; their final response doesn't have to be what you determine to be the perfect finish. Rather, focus on having the kids think, and accept their ideas.

2.5 Appreciating Someone Who Thinks Differently Than You Do

Content Objective: Apply ideas about peace to a current situation at home or school. Discuss ways to make ourselves feel peaceful, and discuss how to foster peace in the classroom and other situations. Make a final statement and refer to texts to make the argument clear.

Application is the fifth dimension of the cubing project, and arguing for or against an idea is the sixth dimension. This lesson incorporates both the application of ideas and the argument for those ideas together in a final presentation of the cubing chart.

Language Objective: Use varied language for effectiveness in making a point, describe with examples in writing, speak in front of a large group, and explicitly reference texts when making a point.

Response: Complete the cubing chart with the six dimensions filled in and give a final oral presentation of the chart to the class.

1. Discuss Depth of Acceptance

Talk with the class about how tolerance can be for groups of people, as *So Far from the Sea* (Bunting 1998) showed, and how tolerance begins in our classrooms and schools, as discussed with *Chrysanthemum* (Henkes 1996a) Tolerance also includes simply accepting that people are different from one another and that peace can occur when we don't just tolerate, but accept people who think differently than we do. Give examples of acceptance from current classroom, school, or world issues. Elicit discussion from the group, focusing on how true acceptance of another person is when you can accept her ideas, without trying to change them, because that is what she believes or thinks, and therefore you can appreciate that person for who she is. Good examples for young students in this area might be about how friends like different types of pizza (how do you compromise at the pizza parlor?) and how siblings argue because they think their way is always right.

2. Discuss Cubing Diagram

Bring out the cubing diagram from the first lesson and show how four of the dimensions have been addressed, but the dimensions of *application* and *argument* have not been completed. Explain that to finish up the unit of study on tolerance, the students are going to apply their ideas to current situations at school or in the world and decide how they could solve these problems through acceptance and tolerance. Explain to the kids that each of them needs to think of a final point for his argument and that they will be sharing and defending their ideas in front of the class or a group.

3. Building Background Knowledge

In order for students to apply ideas of tolerance, and create a final argument, they need further experiences with discussing everyday situations and analyzing these situations in a group. The process of reading a book and thinking about the characters' actions and how the characters accepted others, tolerated situations, or were not respectful of others gives the class multiple opportunities to analyze, think, share ideas, and formulate an opinion. Students need a lot of practice with this step before filling in their cubing diagrams and sharing them with a group. There are many books that would work well for this lesson; see Figure 9.4 for suggestions.

Other lessons for older or more advanced students might include

- Do We Have Peace in Our City, Country, and World?
  Objective: Define peace in multiple contexts and give facts to support opinions. Create a "Yes/No" fact chart using students' knowledge of local and global events; use newspapers, the Internet, and other multimedia sources for information. (See Appendix A for a sample "Yes/No" fact chart.)
- Do Peaceful Countries Go to War?
  Objective: This lesson works best with middle school students. Students can use a "Yes/No" fact chart to decide if it is possible to have peace and war occurring in a country simultaneously. They can base their opinions on world event information gathered from multimedia sources and newspapers.
- Interpreting Truth in Texts
  Objective: Recognize nonfiction sources that have factual information versus sources that may not report factual information. Note and discuss points in text that seem fake or too unbelievable to be real. Explore student-appropriate websites and evaluate them for authenticity. Create a list of accurate and reliable sources for research.
- Identifying Fact and Opinion
  Teaching Point: Recognize fact in expository texts and contrast with opinion. Explore differences between facts and opinions in primary source reading selections, biographies, and persuasive feature articles. Teach text-previewing strategies to help students identify statements that might be opinions of the author or of persons who were interviewed. Text previewing can be taught through the examination of headings and locational devices (e.g., information boxes and indexes) (Moss 2003).

■ Reading for Fact, Writing for Emphasis

Objective: Help students connect ideas they develop while reading to their writing. Show students how to use a text connections chart (see Appendix A) to note connections they make to the topic of peace and subtopics of tolerance and acceptance. Then model for students how to use the information in this graphic organizer to make their written statements stronger and more precise. This lesson can be used in conjunction with the lesson titled "Appreciating Someone Who Thinks Differently Than You Do." The students can make explicit references to texts in their analysis using their thoughts on the text connections organizer. Model how to connect their ideas from reading, which are on the text connections sheet, to written statements to make their final written work a blend of their ideas and supporting information from texts.

Content Study: Civil Rights (see Figure 9.5)

3.1 Developing Academic Language for Civil Rights

Content Objective: Develop understanding of three tier two vocabulary words (see Chapter 5 for a discussion of tier two vocabulary words) related to civil rights. Foster incidental learning of other words connected to the civil rights movement.

Language Objective: Develop vocabulary by actively connecting new information to information previously learned (*TESOL Standards* 1997).

Response: Three semantic webs on chart paper created through whole-group discussion.

1. Introduce the Purpose of the Minilesson

"We are beginning a new unit of study. This unit is on the civil rights movement. When thinking about this time in history, I realized that it will be important for you to know and understand the vocabulary we will see and hear in the books we are going to explore about civil rights."

2. Instruction Point: Introduce Vocabulary

"Today we are going to think about three words and brainstorm what we know about these words. The words we are going to focus on are *rights*, *responsibility*, and *freedom*. Together we are going to think of what other words we know that connect to these words and we are going to write these on our semantic web. During the weeks that we are studying civil rights, we are going to encounter other words that connect to our understanding of these three words and we can add them to our charts to help us learn more words and help us learn more about civil rights. Words help us connect ideas together."

Put up the first semantic web with the word *rights* in the middle. (See Appendix A for an example of a semantic web.) Discuss; add words that students think of. A few key words that connect with *rights* are *privileges*,

LANGUAGE WORKSHOP

Content Study: Civil Rights

Charts and Graphics to Aid Language Development	Lesson Choices	Teaching Focus	Books and Resources
Three semantic webs for *rights, responsibility,* and *freedom* "Thick and Thin Questions" T-chart "Leader's Feelings" chart Event time line	Developing Academic Language for Civil Rights Thick and Thin Questions and Understanding Text Viewpoints of Famous Civil Rights Leaders What Does Discrimination Feel Like? Understanding Different Viewpoints Developing an Event Time Line	Develop understanding of tier two vocabulary words related to civil rights: *rights, responsibility,* and *freedom.* Develop vocabulary by actively connecting new information to information previously learned. Explore ideas about civil rights by asking questions of the text. Learn the difference between thin questions, which are answered in the text, and thick questions, which require inference. Use thick and thin question to help students understand meaning of texts relating to human rights and civil rights. Develop an understanding of how people might have felt during the civil rights movement by researching the stories and backgrounds of civil rights leaders. Evaluate behavior of people in different events, interpret a political context, and explain ideas orally and in writing. Develop an understanding of how discrimination feels by inferring the feelings of children in various picture books and nonfiction texts.	Bridges, Ruby. 1999. *Through My Eyes.* Coleman, Evelyn. 1999. *White Socks Only.* Donovan, Sandra. 2004. *Rosa Parks: An African American Biography.* McGill, Alice. 1999. *Molly Bannaky.* McKissack, Patricia. 2001. *Goin' Someplace Special.* Morrison, Toni. 2002. *The Big Box.* Soentpiet, Chris K. 2000. *Momma, Where Are You From?* Vaughan, Marcia. 2001. *The Secret to Freedom.* Wiles, Deborah. 2001. *Freedom Summer.* Williams, Sherley Anne. 1992. *Working Cotton.* Woodson, Jacqueline. 2001. *The Other Side.*

FIGURE 9.5   Unit-of-Study Design Sheet: Civil Rights

human rights, civil rights, civil liberties, benefit, enjoy, withheld, honor, special, elite, advantage, social status, restricted, advantage, exempt. While writing the words on the chart, talk about the students' thinking and the connections they see. Also talk about your thinking, about what other words mean, and about how you connect words together. Focus on making your thinking transparent while showing students how your brain connects ideas and concepts together. Repeat this work with semantic webs for *responsibility* and *freedom.*

3.3 Thick and Thin Questions and Understanding Text: Day One

Content Objective: Explore ideas about civil rights by asking questions of the text. Learn the difference between thin questions, which are answered in the text, and thick questions, which require inference.

1. Purpose of the Minilesson
Gather students in the class meeting area. Tell them, "As we read and think, it is important to learn how to ask questions while we are reading. Asking questions helps us understand the information in our reading; it also helps us understand important events in history. As we think about the civil rights movement, it is important to understand how people were treated and how they were discriminated against based upon their skin color."

2. Instruction Point
"There are two types of questions that we can ask as we read and think about our reading. One is a thin question. Thin questions are questions that are answered by facts, ideas, or opinions that are right there in the text. The other type of question is a thick question. Thick questions cannot be answered with information right there in the text. These questions require you to make inferences to come up with possible answers. It is important to distinguish between thick questions and thin questions to learn to think critically about our reading. When we think critically about what we read, we ponder not only what the author is saying but how the event or information impacts our lives or reflects on something important in our world.

"As we think about our reading today, we are going to write questions on sticky notes. I want you to try to write thick and thin questions. I'm going to give you three sticky notes, and while I'm reading, I want you to write down the questions that come to your mind on the sticky notes." Pass out notes and clipboards so that students can write easily on their laps.

Read *The Big Box*, by Toni Morrison (2002). Pause in places that invite students to think or invite you to think aloud for students regarding the meaning of what is happening to the characters. Help students focus on writing thick and thin questions. It isn't important at this point that they write only thick questions; you want to help them learn the difference between the two question types.

3. Share and Discuss

After reading the books, have several students share their sticky notes. Discuss whether their questions are thick or thin. Finish the discussion by having students think about the meaning of the book *The Big Box*. If they struggled with thick questions, ask: "What happened to the children in the box? Why were they there? Why didn't the children have rights?"

3.3 Thick and Thin Questions and Understanding Text: Day Two

Content Objective: Use thick and thin questions to help students understand meaning of texts relating to human rights and civil rights. (Civil rights are public or social rights and human rights relate to treatment of humans in general. For example, someone can have human rights but not civil rights, although the two concepts are intertwined.)

Prepare a large T-chart on butcher paper or a chart pad. Label the top of the T-chart "Thin Questions" and "Thick Questions." (See Appendix A for an "Asking Questions" chart.) Choose a text from the recommended books for the civil rights study (see Figure 9.5, page 117).

1. Introduce the Purpose of the Minilesson

"Yesterday you wrote thick and thin questions for the book we read, *The Big Box*. Today we are going to read another book related to civil rights and write thick and thin questions again. Remember that thin questions can be answered in the text, and thick questions have to be answered by our thinking. We use clues in the text to answer thick questions. We have to make inferences."

2. Read and Discuss

While reading, pause at thoughtful points in the text and have students write questions on sticky notes. About halfway through the book, stop reading and ask students to come up and place their sticky notes on the T-chart under "Thick" or "Thin." Discuss each question and decide if it is under the correct heading. If it is misplaced, move the note. Don't worry if the students are not very good at writing thick questions yet; this ability comes with practice. After reading the book, add any remaining sticky notes to the chart. Discuss the questions and the students' thinking behind them. Prompt the students to think about why they asked a question and if the answer is right there in the text or not. Move sticky notes under the correct heading if necessary.

3. Wrap Up Thinking

While examining the thick and thin questions, encourage students to discuss the meaning of the book you chose to read and the connection of the book to civil rights. Hopefully this conversation will occur naturally with the exploration of their thick and thin questions. If not, encourage students to elaborate on their understanding. Add their ideas about the book to the bottom of the T-chart. You can write on the chart or use a sentence strip. Sentence strips work well to highlight their overall analysis; the strip of paper sets off their final thoughts and provides organization to the chart.

3.4 Viewpoints of Famous Civil Rights Leaders

Content Objective: Develop an understanding of how people might have felt during the civil rights movement by researching the stories and backgrounds of civil rights leaders.

Language Objective: Evaluate behavior of people in different events, interpret a political context, and explain ideas orally and in writing.

Prepare sticky notes and a large chart with "Leader's Feelings" on one side of the chart and "Our Thinking" on the other side. You'll need at least one copy of *Through My Eyes*, by Ruby Bridges (1999), and *Rosa Parks: An African American Biography*, by Sandra Donovan (2004), to teach the lesson; multiple copies are preferable.

1. Purpose of the Minilesson

"There are many people who helped ensure that African Americans are treated equally in our country and world. In fact, the civil rights movement that led to the desegregation of the United States led to awareness of civil rights around the world. For the next couple of days we are going to explore two people who were leaders. Although they were ordinary people just like us, they were leaders because in their own way they set out to make a difference. One of these people is Rosa Parks and the other is Ruby Bridges."

2. Instruction Point

This lesson will spread out over several days in order for students to explore, discuss, and compare ideas and themes across both books and then offer ideas for the class chart (this will be a group consensus chart—the students should discuss ideas and agree on the statements written on the chart).

First, break the class into small groups and pass out multiple copies of each book (if available) along with sticky notes. Discuss with students how they should write on the sticky notes information they think will be important to remember. They can keep the notes in their language notebooks or in the copy of the book. Read each book separately and spend at least one full language workshop session discussing the ideas in the first book before moving on to the second one.

After reading both books, help students explore the feelings of the civil rights leaders. Using the chart labeled "Leader's Feelings" and "Our Thoughts," lead a discussion with the kids about what they think Ruby Bridges and Rosa Parks might have felt. Add specific details to the chart to model using specificity in language and using facts to back up statements.

FIGURE 9.6 Claudia's Synthesis About Ruby Bridges

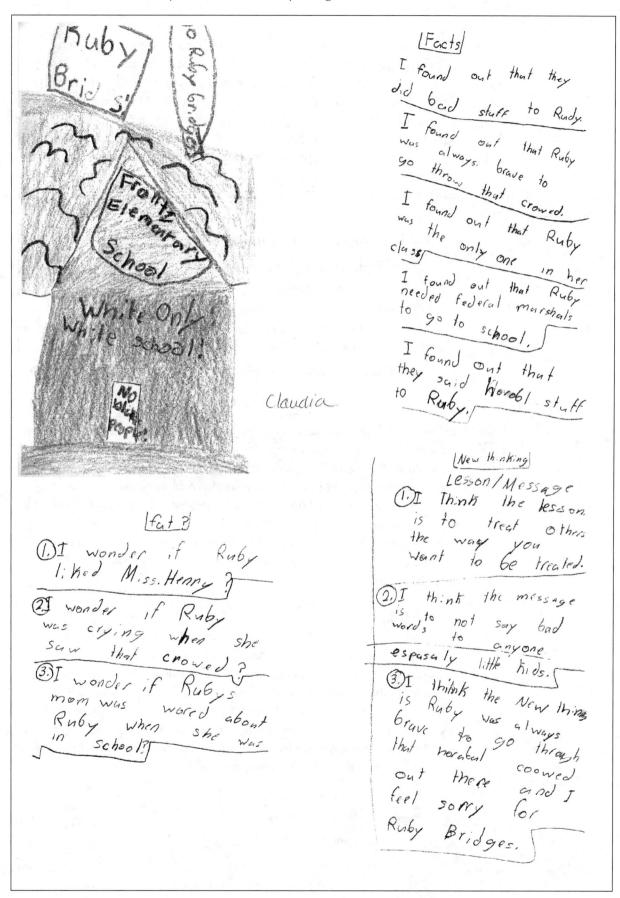

Ruby Bridges

To Ruby Bridges

Frontz Elementary School

White Only White school!!

NO blacks popl.

Claudia

Facts

I found out that they did bad stuff to Ruby.

I found out that Ruby was always, brave to go throw that crowed.

I found out that Ruby was the only one in her class

I found out that Ruby needed federal marshals to go to school.

I found out that they said horobl stuff to Ruby.

fat ?

① I wonder if Ruby liked Miss. Henry ?

② I wonder if Ruby was crying when she saw that crowed ?

③ I wonder if Rubys mom was wored about Ruby when she was in school ?

New thinking

Lesson / Message

① I Think the lesson is to treat others the way you want to be treated.

② I think the message is to not say bad words to anyone espasaly little kids.

③ I think the New thing is Ruby was always brave to go through that horabal coowed out there and I feel sorry for Ruby Bridges.

After discussing the books and the feelings of Ruby Bridges and Rosa Parks, continue to read and infer the feelings and characteristics of other civil rights leaders. After studying several people of the civil rights movement, Sharon Mayo at Lee Richmond School in Hanford, California, had her third graders write about what they had learned and what they thought the leaders felt. Claudia chose to write about Ruby Bridges; you can see her synthesis of ideas in Figure 9.6. She listed the facts that she learned, and on the bottom right side of the paper, she listed her thoughts about the issues Bridges faced.

3.5 What Does Discrimination Feel Like?

Content Objective: Develop an understanding of how discrimination feels by inferring the feelings of children in various picture books and nonfiction texts.

Language Objective: Connect new information to information already learned, and express feelings orally and in writing.

Materials: One copy of *The Other Side*, by Jacqueline Woodson (2001).

1. Purpose of the Minilesson
"For several days we have been discussing discrimination. There are times we are all discriminated against, for one reason or another, and it doesn't feel good. For many years, children weren't allowed to play together because of the color of their skin. That sounds odd to us today, but for a long time it was a reality that not all children understood; in fact, I have trouble understanding it myself. We are going to read a book today, and while we read it, I want you to pretend to be one of the characters in the book. And while you are that character, I want you to think about how it might feel to be discriminated against."

2. Instruction Point
The class will need to make inferences about the characters' feelings. Have students work in pairs or trios. Ask them to talk about their thoughts at specific points in the text. Pause your reading and ask the class, "How do you think the character feels? How would you feel if it were you?" Then have the students discuss in their groups. At the end of the lesson, have the groups report how they believe it feels to be discriminated against; they can add details from any experiences they have had. Possible stopping points in the text include the following passages.

Page 1: "Don't climb over that fence . . ."

Page 3: "Maybe yes. Maybe no."

Page 4: "It's not polite."

Page 7: "I felt free."

Page 9: ". . . looking at each other, smiling."

LANGUAGE WORKSHOP

Content Study: Diversity

Charts and Graphics to Aid Language Development	Lesson Choices	Teaching Focus	Books and Resources
"What Is Diversity" chart	What Diversity Means to Ourselves, Our School, Our City—*Explore local cultural groups.*	Develop an understanding of similarities and differences between cultural groups.	Brinckloe, Julie. 1986. *Fireflies.*
Graphic depicting ethnic/racial groups represented in the school and classroom	Discovering How We Are the Same and Different—*Value others and treat others with respect.*	Understand various cultural and ethnic groups represented in the school and community.	Bunting, Eve. 1993. *Fly Away Home.*
T-chart labeled "Similarities" and "Differences"	Appreciating Cultural and Ethnic Backgrounds—*Exposing students to foods, customs, and values of different cultural groups.*	Become familiar with traditions and values of other peoples.	Climo, Shirley. 1993. *The Korean Cinderella.*
	Accepting Cultural and Diverse Viewpoints—*Modeling how to take the perspectives of others.*	Develop respect for people who come from different backgrounds.	Climo, Shirley. 1999. *The Persian Cinderella.*
	Similarities Between Cultures' Values, Celebrations, and Entertainment—*Connect students to the similarities between people to build respect.*	Learn to listen to others' stories and ideas to understand fellow classmates' actions and beliefs.	Coburn, Jewell Reinhart, with Tzexa Chertz. 1996. *Jouanah, A Hmong Cinderella.*
	What Can We Learn from Someone Different from Ourselves?—*Discuss how we learn from the experiences of others.*	Develop respect for everyone in the school.	Davidson, Margaret. 1995. *Helen Keller.*
	Ways to Foster Respect in Our Lives and the Greater World—*Instill a need to "get along" in the classroom community and model different ways of showing respect.*	Reduce the need to bully someone who is different, or comes from a different background.	Feelings, Tom. 2004. *I Saw Your Face.*
			Henkes, Kevin. 1997. *Chester's Way.*
			Hoffman, Mary. 2000. *Boundless Grace.*
			Holman, Sandy Lynne. 1998. *Grandpa, Is Everything Black Bad?*
			Lorbiecki, Marybeth. 2000. *Sister Anne's Hands.*
			Louie, Ai-Ling. 1982. *Yeh Shen: A Cinderella Story from China.*
			Miller, Phillip J. 2001. *We All Sing with the Same Voice.*
			Oughton, Jerrie. 1992. *How the Stars Fell into the Sky: A Navajo Legend.*
			Polacco, Patricia. 2000. *The Butterfly.*
			Silverman, Erica. 1999. *Raisel's Riddle.*
			Thomas, Marlo. 2002. *Free to Be You and Me.*
			Turner, Ann. 1995. *Nettie's Trip South.*
			Weiss, George David. 1995. *What a Wonderful World.*
			Winter, Jeanette. 2005. *The Librarian of Basra.*

FIGURE 9.7   Unit-of-Study Design Sheet: Diversity

Page 10: "I didn't care."

Page 13: "Someday."

Additional lessons might include

■ Understanding Different Viewpoints
Objective: Develop the ability to take another person's point of view and then explore an issue from two perspectives. Create a class chart listing two to four significant people or groups in the civil rights movement. For example, the class might explore the viewpoint of Ruby Bridges' parents and the parents of white children at William Frantz Public School. Another way of examining multiple viewpoints is to discuss political cartoons or art from the era. In *Through My Eyes*, by Ruby Bridges, there is a picture by Norman Rockwell on page 25 that invites discussion of multiple viewpoints.

Another text that works well for discussing viewpoint and rights is *I Dream of Peace: Images of War by Children of Former Yugoslavia*, by James P. Grant (1994). This book shows the perspective of children in war.

FIGURE 9.8   Sharon's Class Chart on Helen Keller

Another lesson in this unit might include:

■ Developing an Event Time Line
Objective: Research important events during the civil rights movement
by using a variety of nonfiction texts at various reading levels. Take
notes on important events and create a time line chronicling the
moments that changed segregation laws and norms. This project can be
done as a whole group. Have students write their events on multicolored
sentence strips, placing the date on the left side of the strip and the event
detail on the right side of the strip. Encourage students to describe the
event in their own words to help them summarize the important points
into a sentence or two. The time line is effective when displayed on a
wall where students can visually connect events, ideas, and themes
together.

Sharon Mayo also explores theme within a diversity unit each year.
Figures 9.8 and 9.9 are examples of student thinking from the walls in
Sharon's class when she read *Helen Keller* (Davidson 1995) in her workshop as part of her diversity unit. Figure 9.9 is a close-up of one of the
student's thinking; she wrote, "I think she meant that you can't see and
touch in heaven, but you only touch and see in your wonderful heart."

FIGURE 9.9   Student Thinking on Helen Keller

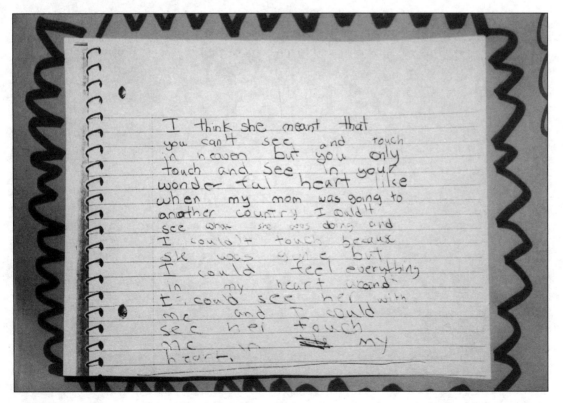

FIGURE 9.10 Sharon's Class Chart on *Nettie's Trip South*

Figure 9.10 is another example from Sharon's diversity unit. The picture shows how Sharon's students posted their thinking after meeting in groups. This poster was related to the book *Nettie's Trip South* (Turner 1995).

CHAPTER TEN

Language Lessons Focusing on Strategy Instruction

Strategy Study: Making Great Connections and Developing Schema

The complete unit is shown in the unit-of-study planning sheet (Figure 10.1). This unit is designed to deepen students' understanding of connecting and responding to text orally and in writing. If your students do not have any experience with discussing or thinking of text connections, you may prefer to begin with a unit of study that breaks down making connections into small steps. If you teach young children, or children new to English, it may be more appropriate to teach the Making Connections unit first (see Figure 10.2). An excellent source for various graphic organizers, text structures, and strategies can be found in the *Reader's Handbook: A Student Guide for Reading and Learning*, by Robb, Klemp, and Schwartz (2002).

1.1 Comprehension and Connections: Adding "Why" to Our Work

1. Purpose of the Minilesson

"For a while we have been discussing and recording our ideas and connections while we read. Now, it is important for us to be more thoughtful in our connections. We need to go beyond 'This text reminds me of my mom' or 'I have blue sneakers like the character in the book.' We need to make connections that make us think deeply about the story line, the characters' thoughts and actions, or the problem and solution in the story.

"Let me show you what I mean. In the book *Circle of Thanks*, by Susi Gregg Fowler (1998), on page 2 the mother helps a small animal. Now, I have never been to the tundra, so I don't have a connection to the tundra, but I have been to the mountains and I know the mountains are very

LANGUAGE WORKSHOP

Strategy Study: Making Great Connections and Developing Schema

Charts and Graphics to Aid Language Development	Lesson Choices	Teaching Focus	Books and Resources
"Making Meaningful Connections" chart	Comprehension and Connections: Adding "Why" to Our Work	Find connections that make us think deeply about the story line, the characters' thoughts and actions, or the problem and solution in the story.	Cooney, Barbara. 1999. *Basket Moon.*
Monitoring book tabs (see Appendix A)	Connections to Quick Flashes of Information from the World	Share your connections with your partner, but most importantly, add *why* you made the connection.	Dragonwagon, Crescent. 1990. *Home Place.*
Definition chart: "What Is a Quick Flash?"	Connections to Quick Flashes in Our Lives	Sometimes when I read, a picture flashes across my mind; this kind of picture usually pops up when I read something that triggers a memory. It is important to pay attention to those quick flashes that pop up while we read.	Fleischman, Paul. 1999. *Weslandia.*
"Connecting to the News" chart	Expand Language and Understanding		Fowler, Susi Gregg. 1998. *Circle of Thanks.*
"Language to Use in Partner Share" chart	What We Read Changes What We Know		Gandos, Paul. 2001. *Joey Pigza Swallowed the Key.*
	Common Language for Discussing Connections		Hesse, Karen. 1993. *Lester's Dog*
	Great Readers Read and Think at the Same Time	Focus on those quick flashes of memory while reading fiction.	Hobbie, Hollie. 2003. *Toot and Puddle.*
	Making Meaningful Connections	When we are working together it is important for you to know how to begin a discussion, address a partner, restate information, add your ideas to the ideas of another person, and disagree politely.	Jenkins, Emily. 2004. *My Favorite Thing (According to Alberta).*
	Responding Thoughtfully		Knoll, Virginia. 1995. *Fireflies, Peach Pies & Lullabies.*
			Lasky, Kathryn. 1988. *Sea Swan.*
			Lee, Milly. 1997. *Nim and the War Effort.*
			MacLachlan, Patricia. 1980. *Through Grandpa's Eyes.*
			Munson, Derek. 2000. *Enemy Pie.*
			Napoli, Donna Jo. 2001. *Albert.*
			Pinkney, Gloria Jean. 1994. *The Sunday Outing.*
			Ryan, Pam Munoz. 2004. *Becoming Naomi Leon.*
			Teacher Created Materials. 2000. "Hotshots: Kids Who Are Getting the Most Out of Sports." *Write Time for Kids.*
			Zolotow, Charlotte. 2002. *If You Listen.*

FIGURE 10.1 Unit-of-Study Sheet: Making Great Connections and Developing Schema

LANGUAGE WORKSHOP

Strategy Study: Making Connections

Charts and Graphics to Aid Language Development	Lesson Choices	Teaching Focus	Books and Resources
Charts listing the qualities of each type of connection	Great Readers Think While Reading—*All good readers think while reading.*	Good readers make connections between their lives and what they are reading.	Best, Cari. 2001. *Shrinking Violet.*
Charts with teacher- and student-written models of text connections	Making Connections to Text—*Good readers make connections to text while reading to aid comprehension.*	There are three types of connections: text-to-self, text-to-text, and text-to-world.	Finchler, Judy. 1998. *Miss Malarky Won't Be in Today.*
	What Is a Text-to-Self Connection?—*Model and describe text-to-self connections.*	Making connections helps readers comprehend, analyze, evaluate, and synthesize information in texts.	Fitzpatrick, Marie Louise. 2000. *Lizzy and Skunk.* Heo, Yumi. 2002. *Sometimes I'm Bombaloo.* Howe, James. 1999. *Horace and Morris but Mostly Dolores.*
	How to Record a Text-to-Self Connection—*Model how to write a text-to-self connection in a response journal or log.*	Explicit instruction in text connections helps culturally and linguistically diverse students pay attention to their thinking and develop awareness of their comprehension processes.	Inkpen, Mick. 1995. *Nothing.* Kilborne, Sarah S. 1994. *Peach and Blue.* Middleton, Charlotte. 2001. *Tabitha's Terrifically Tough Tooth.*
	What Is a Text-to-Text Connection?—*Model and describe text-to-text connections.*	Writing is the highest level of language use and reflects skills in analyzing thinking and effectively representing thought in print.	Polacco, Patricia. 1990. *Thundercake.*
	How to Record a Text-to-Text Connection—*Model how to write a text-to-text connection.*	Discussing text connections with peers provides opportunities for students to practice English in an academic discourse.	Schuett, Stacey. 1995. *Somewhere in the World Right Now.*
	What Is a Text-to-World Connection?—*Model and describe text-to-world connections.*		Soto, Gary. 1993. *Too Many Tamales.*
	How to Record a Text-to-World Connection—*Model how to write a text-to-world connection.*		Wood, Audrey, and Mark Teague. 1998. *Sweet Dream Pie.*
	Sharing Our Connections with Others—*Discuss and practice how to talk about books with a partner.*		*The lessons for this unit of study are not written out in the book. This design sheet lists the objectives for the lessons under "Teaching Focus," and a short explanation of each lesson is given after the lesson title.*

FIGURE 10.2 Unit-of-Study Sheet: Making Connections

different from the city. So, when I read this page, I have a text-to-self connection—I think about how different it would be to live in the mountains than in the city. I also remember how there are people in the city that help animals. So, although I live in the city, I do have a text-to-self connection to what happens when the mother helps the otter pup. I have been to the animal shelter and there are many people there that help abandoned animals. I also have a text-to-world connection to this page because I know that there are groups of people that help animals. Recently in the news, there were scientists who helped some stranded dolphins find their way back to the sea.

"So today when I am reading aloud, you are going to share your connections with your partner, but most importantly, you are going to add *why* you made the connections. Just like I explained how the mother helping the otter pup reminded me of people helping animals in the city, I want you to tell your neighbor *why* you made your connection. Tell the thinking behind your connection."

2. Teaching Sequence

After introducing the purpose of the lesson, show the book for the day and begin reading. Stop reading from time to time and have students turn to a partner and share their connections. Make sure to emphasize the *why*, or the deep thinking behind the connection. At the end of the workshop, encourage the students to share some of their connections with the whole class.

1.2 Connections to Quick Flashes of Information from the World

1. Purpose of the Minilesson

"Sometimes when I read, a picture flashes across my mind. This type of picture usually pops up when I read something that triggers a memory. It is important to pay attention to those 'quick flashes' that pop up while we read. At first, you might not even notice them, thinking that you are getting distracted from your reading, but what is actually happening is your brain is making connections to what you are reading, and a flash of a memory pops up.

"Look at this Write Time for Kids text titled 'Hotshots: Kids Who Are Getting the Most Out of Sports.'" (This piece comes inside the Write Time for Kids kit by Teacher Created Materials [2002]. This text is on an overhead. Any good nonfiction piece on sports or another child-centered event would work for this lesson.) "This text is about three students and how they excel at sports." (Here I would show the piece on the overhead that has three pictures of students playing their sport.) "When I read how the girl Shadisha loves to play tennis, and has won the title of number one player in the eastern United States, a quick flash of a memory came across my mind. I remembered trying to hit the tennis ball a few times at a park near my house, but I wasn't successful. I think tennis is difficult, but here is a student who excels at tennis. That quick flash also reminded me of a tennis match I watched on TV between two famous tennis players.

"When I read the information in 'Hotshots,' I connect to things I know about sports. I also learn new information because I didn't know students that young could earn tennis titles. The quick flash I had in my head helped me make meaning of what I read."

2. Teaching Sequence
When students connect to text, they connect new learning to concepts and ideas they already understand. This is how students develop new concepts, or schemata. By focusing on their connections and thinking deeply about new ideas, they understand more about their reading and about their world.

After introducing this lesson, share a different nonfiction piece and encourage students to share their quick flashes that occur during the read-aloud. When sharing nonfiction with the whole group, it is optimal for all students to be able to see the text well in order to process the pictures and the headings; individual copies or a copy of the text on an overhead work well for this. Encourage students to pay attention to their thinking and to their flashes of memory, and then have them discuss what they are thinking about and how the information in the article expanded what they already knew.

1.3 Connections to Quick Flashes in Our Lives

Purpose of the Minilesson and Teaching Sequence
The purpose of this minilesson and the teaching sequence are the same as for lesson two except that this lesson demonstrates how to focus on those quick flashes of memory while reading fiction. When reading nonfiction, children connect their experiences to information, and when reading fiction children should connect their lives to the lives of the characters. Sometimes we identify with a character; sometimes we are annoyed or repulsed by a character. It is important for students to focus on their thoughts and feelings in order to analyze how they are connecting to a fiction text.

One book that works well for this lesson with younger children, or with students new to English, is *Toot and Puddle*, by Hollie Hobbie (2003). A book that works well for older children is *Enemy Pie*, by Derek Munson (2000). There are also many chapter books that work as a read-aloud. When teaching a chapter book, like *Becoming Naomi Leon*, by Pam Munoz Ryan (2004), or *Joey Pigza Swallowed the Key*, by Paul Gandos (2001), you model the quick flashes that come to your mind while you read, and ask your students to share their flashes and subsequent thinking. They can share orally and in writing by using response notebooks. By focusing on their thinking, children will learn to make connections beyond surface-level, shallow connections. Deeper connections will help them understand their reading, and will give them a springboard for discussion. Through discussing connections, they develop language while they practice an important literacy strategy.

1.4 Expand Language and Understanding

1. Purpose of the Minilesson

"When we are working together it is important for you to know how to begin a discussion, address a partner, restate information, add your ideas to the ideas of another person, and disagree politely. Today, we are going to practice some of the things we might say so that when we are working together, figuring out how to say something won't get in our way; we will already know *how* to say something.

"Let me give you an example. Yesterday we were talking about the book *My Favorite Thing (According to Alberta)* (Jenkins 2004). I mentioned what my favorite ice-cream flavor is, and then Jose said to me, 'Oh, cookies and cream ice cream is my favorite, too.' Today when we are talking with each other, I want you to practice listening to what your partner says and then responding. It isn't good enough if we are all talking but not *listening* to each other. Only when we listen can we have a conversation, and dialogue, about an important issue."

2. Teaching Sequence

Discuss with your students how they feel when someone really listens to their opinions, and during the discussion list important ideas that come up. Create class norms and values around talk and listening and then try to stick to these ideals. It helps English learners to have sentence springboards, like *I agree with _____ because _____* or *This information in the book _____ is similar to the ideas we are talking about because _____.* When partner sharing, they can start with *My partner and I think that _____. We think this because _____.* See Figure 10.3 for an example of how students' thinking about books can be displayed to teach and reteach pertinent strategies. Figure 10.4 shows an example of how your minilesson can model for students how to think about their reading and discussion and then write more down in order to capture their thinking.

Additional lessons might include

- What We Read Changes What We Know
  Objective: Rely on background knowledge to comprehend text, develop domain knowledge and make meaning.
- Common Language for Discussing Connections
  Objective: Model effective language use when describing, evaluating, analyzing, and synthesizing texts. Show students how to talk about their reading.
- Great Readers Read and Think at the Same Time
  Objective: Develop ability to focus on meaning by using multiple strategies to understand text.

FIGURE 10.3 Responding to Books Wall

FIGURE 10.4 "Using Our Sticky Notes to Write More" Teaching Chart

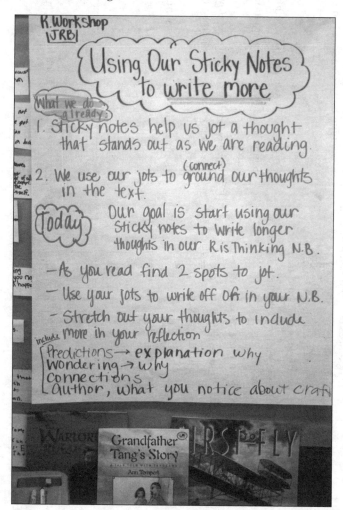

LANGUAGE WORKSHOP

Strategy Study: Synthesizing Text Through Retelling

Charts and Graphics to Aid Language Development	Lesson Choices	Teaching Focus	Books and Resources
Retelling chart	How to Retell	Improve comprehension and improve thinking skills.	Arnold, Marsha Diane. 1998. *The Pumpkin Runner.*
Plot line chart	Recognizing Character, Plot, and Setting	Recall story events by understanding what the author is telling in order to focus on what is happening to the characters and the action in the story.	Barron, T. A. 2004. *High as a Hawk.*
Retelling nonfiction chart	Differences Between Retelling and Summarizing		Chall, Marsha Wilson. 1998. *Rupa Raises the Sun.*
Story map	Good Nonfiction Summaries	Learn how to summarize.	Davis, Lucilee. 1997. *Cesar Chavez.*
"Big Idea" chart	Synthesize Ideas and Information	Compare a summary to a retelling.	Henkes, Kevin. 1988. *Chester's Way.*
Summarizing sheet	Summarize: Put It In Your Own Words	Synthesize ideas and information in order to be succinct.	Numeroff, Laura. 2004. *Beatrice Doesn't Want To.*
Nonfiction summary notes	Summarizing Literature	Develop ability to break text down into parts.	Oberman, Sheldon. 1994. *The Always Prayer Shawl.*
	Summarizing Nonfiction	Read a portion of text and then think about what that portion of text *means.*	Osborne, Mary Pope. 2002. *The Brave Little Seamstress.*
	Evaluating a Novel or Story	Connect ideas in the text to something already known.	Rosa-Casnova, Sylvia. 1997. *Mama Provi and the Pot of Rice.*
	Evaluating Nonfiction		Soto, Gary. 1993. *Too Many Tamales.*
	Synthesize: Put the Ideas Together		Stewart, Sarah. 2004. *The Friend.*
			Magazines:
			Your Big Backyard
			Ranger Rick

FIGURE 10.5 Unit-of-Study Sheet: Summarizing and Synthesizing Text

- Making Meaningful Connections

  Objective: Think about what the text means. Connect background knowledge to ideas or theme in text. Discuss concepts learned in domain/content areas.
- Responding Thoughtfully

  Objective: Participate in oral or written response by selecting vocabulary carefully, speaking clearly, and listening to ideas offered by peers.

Strategy Study: Summarizing and Synthesizing Text

2.1 How to Retell (See Figure 10.5)

1. Purpose of the Minilesson

"When we retell stories, we think carefully about what happened in the beginning, middle, and end of a story. This helps improve our comprehension and our thinking skills. Today we are going to practice how to do a good retelling. Good retellings carefully detail the beginning, middle, and end of a story. The retelling also gives important information to the listener."

2. Teaching Sequence

Kindergarten Through Second Grade: Show students a stoplight that you have drawn or made of paper. Relate the green light to the beginning of the story, the yellow light to the middle of the story, and the red light the end of the story. Have students recount a familiar story and point to the green light when retelling the beginning, the yellow light for the middle, and the red light when retelling the end, or resolution, of the story. Use the graphic to embed sequencing of retelling. This works well for students new to English because they can think of the familiar stoplight symbol while thinking about all the details that go into each section of a book.

Have partners retell a story to each other; then practice retelling a story together as a group. As a follow-up lesson, have the students write a retelling with partners. Retellings are longer than summaries so it can be laborious for students to do an entire retelling on their own. One book that works well for this lesson is *Beatrice Doesn't Want To*, by Laura Numeroff (2004). The beginning, middle, and end are easy to define, as Beatrice learns to read and learns to love the library.

Third Through Eighth Grade: Draw a story retelling chart on the board or chart paper. A story retelling chart lists the following information in order: beginning, event one, event two, event three, and resolution. Read the book *High as a Hawk* (Barron 2004) (or discuss a favorite text) with the class, stopping after each section to discuss the main parts of the book. In *High as a Hawk* a young girl climbs to the top of Longs Peak in Colorado and faces obstacles on the trail and within her; the book is based on a true story. Have students meet in trios and decide which events are part of the beginning, which are part of the middle, and which event is the resolution. These parts are easily identified in *High as a Hawk*. After the class discussion, fill in these events on the story retelling chart. Show students the retelling fiction graphic organizer (see Appendix A), and discuss how the graphic organizer can be used with various texts. Figure 10.6 shows another way of helping students summarize. This chart lists the important story elements for a summary. You can use a chart like the one in Figure 10.6 to model for students how to summarize while describing short snippets of information from the text.

Figure 10.7 shows an example of a plot line. A plot line is another way to help students retell a fictional text. The swell in the middle of the line indicates the climax of the story; the resolution is depicted by a flat line. A plot line helps the children easily see the beginning, middle, and end. The plot lines in Figure 10.7 list the details explaining each part in chronological order.

FIGURE 10.6   Retelling Chart for *Too Many Tamales*

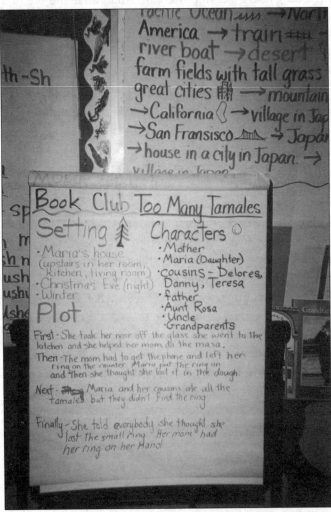

Chapter Ten

FIGURE 10.7 Plot Line Chart

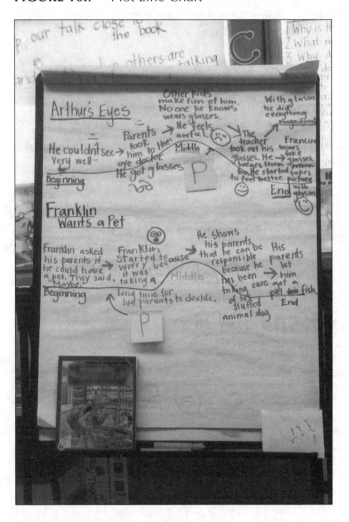

You can also create a line graphic for retelling nonfiction text. A graphic organizer for retelling nonfiction is laid out in a linear fashion but lists information in a different way: introduction, point 1, point 2, point 3, (or as many points as are in the text) conclusion. For a subsequent lesson, you can use the retelling chart for nonfiction found in Appendix A with a feature article from any children's magazine, such as *Your Big Backyard*.

2.2 Recognizing Character, Plot, and Setting

1. Purpose of the Minilesson

"We have been reading and talking about a lot of books in class, and overall, we've done a great job learning to retell. Sometimes it is hard to remember everything in a story, so by using a graphic organizer to help you, you will be able to talk or write about all the parts in the book. One way to remember the story, and understand what the author is telling us, is to focus on what is happening to the characters and the action in the story. We are going to retell using a story map today. When you use a story map you think about the characters, the setting, and the plot. We understand what we've read and why it is important to put all the pieces in our retelling."

2. Teaching Sequence

Show the story map graphic organizer from Appendix A. Explain each part of the story map. The story map lists the important pieces of a retelling. Figure 10.8 shows an example of a story map. This example came from Shana Simpson's classroom at Lee Richmond School in Hanford, California. She filled in the top two sections as she read the beginning of the story.

FIGURE 10.8 *Chester's Way* Story Map

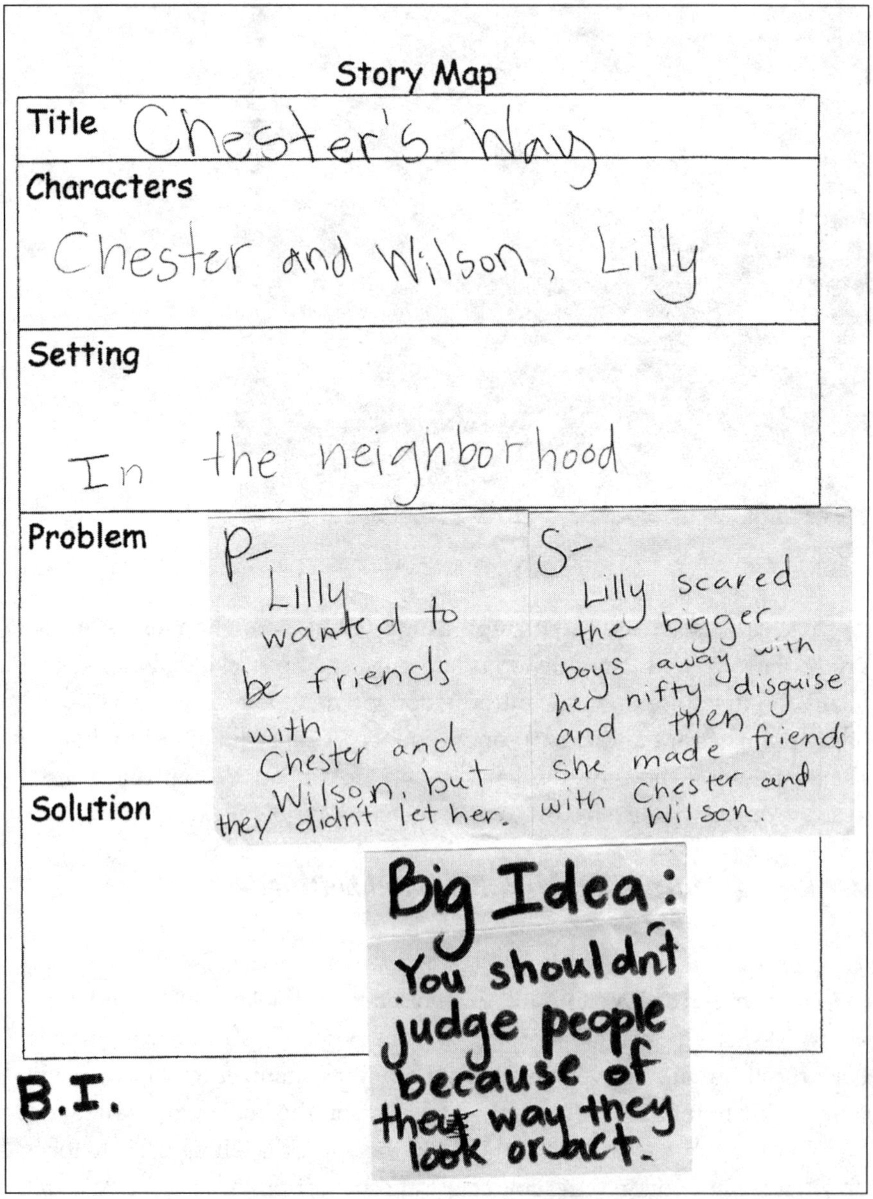

Then, before continuing to read the book, she gave each student a clipboard with three sticky notes. She asked her students to write down the problem and solution of the story when she read those parts. Her students carefully recorded their thinking. Then, Shana had the children tell each other what they had written on their sticky notes. The first few times they completed this activity, Shana used an oversized example of the story map and had the students place their sticky notes on the large chart; later they moved to a smaller paper and filled the graphic in by themselves or with a partner. Figure 10.9 shows the chart she used to model for the students.

2.3 Differences Between Retelling and Summarizing

1. Purpose of the Minilesson
"After you learn to retell, the next step is to learn to summarize. A summary is much shorter than a retelling. Think about it—every time you wanted to share something important that happened to you with your

FIGURE 10.9   "Big Idea" Chart

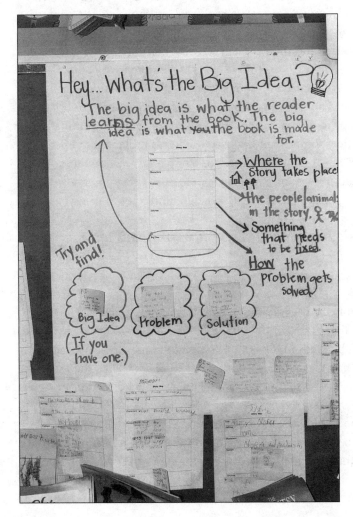

friend, if you gave the long, drawn-out version of the story, your friend would get tired listening. So you have to make your stories shorter. We call this summarizing. Now, retelling is important to help you remember everything that happened in a story, and that might come in really handy when your little sister breaks your mom's favorite dish, and you have to explain how your little sister did it and not you, but often when we tell our thinking, we have to use a short version. When you write a summary, you tell what you think a book is about. You give highlights of the book and you say it in your own words."

2. Teaching Sequence

This is a great opportunity for your students to teach each other through practice and modeling. Split the class into groups of four, and ask the students to bring their book bags or boxes with them to the meeting area. The bags or boxes should be filled with just right reading books and books that you have assigned for reading instruction and practice. Pass out the summarizing sheet (see Appendix A) and explain how students will work together to fill out one or two of these based on the books in their book bags.

As the class experiments with writing ideas in the section titled "What was this book mostly about?" have the groups share their books and their summary statements with the whole group. Highlight a few groups who wrote good summaries and then explain why the summaries are good. The skill of writing or telling a good summary will take time to develop. Be patient! Students have focused on remembering all the facts and details in a book in order to learn and comprehend; now they have to learn to be succinct. Continue to provide many opportunities for the class to summarize fiction and nonfiction books. Pam Pflepsen at Pinedale Elementary School uses this summary sheet in her reading workshop after introducing it to students. They keep these summary sheets in their reading notebooks and Pam uses them as an assessment tool to check reading development.

2.4 Good Nonfiction Summaries Synthesize Ideas and Information

1. Purpose of the Minilesson

"Summarizing nonfiction is very much like summarizing fiction. Good readers read a portion of text and then think about what that portion of text *means*. They hook the ideas in the text to something they already know about. That helps them remember what they read; it also helps the information be meaningful. Let me show you what I mean. When I read *Cesar Chavez* (Davis 1997), I first remembered what I knew about Cesar Chavez. Then I thought about what the book about him was saying; I had to determine what was most important to remember. I was able to figure out what was most important to remember because before I began reading, I thought about how nonfiction books are structured. If you remember, nonfiction has

FIGURE 10.10 Nonfiction Conventions and Information Wall

a different structure than fiction. So, I think about the text structures, and I think about nonfiction conventions, or the features in nonfiction books that help me understand the information. [See Figure 10.10 for an example of a nonfiction convention wall; the wall works well to remind students of important thinking.] Thinking of the text structure and the conventions helps me understand what Cesar Chavez did that was important. And better than that, I can connect the things he did for people to other things I know people have accomplished in our world. Thinking of one thing and adding it to what I know about another thing is called synthesizing."

2. Teaching Sequence

After introducing the lesson, show the chart with the nonfiction text information and remind students how the text structure and conventions can help them make sense of what they read. Write a practice summary on a whiteboard in order to model summarizing for students. Finally, have the students respond in pairs. Choose a biography and have the students talk about what they think is most important to remember while you are reading. After reading, have each group write a summary on their own. Remind them that good summaries have a description of the subject, including the author's viewpoint, and supporting details, words, and phrases. Figure 10.11 is an example from the response journal of one of Doug Carlton's fifth graders at Lee Richmond School in Hanford, California. Renique wrote the main idea/topic on the left and then summarized the meaning of that topic on the right.

Additional lessons might include

- Summarize: Put It in Your Own Words
  Objective: Describe main ideas, events, character, theme, and plot succinctly while expressing author's purpose and/or reader's opinion.
- Summarizing Literature
  Objective: Describe and link information together that affect the theme or plot of a fiction piece.
- Summarizing Nonfiction
  Objective: Locate and integrate information from nonfiction text. Use nonfiction retelling chart in Appendix A to guide student thinking.

FIGURE 10.11   Renique's Nonfiction Summary Notes

04/1	Origins Of English Settlemen
The algonquin people	The algonquin people had lived in peace for many years along the Atlantic coast.
Indians Slaves	The English also knew that Indian slaves in mexico had mined gold and silver for spain.
English Settlement	English merchants wanted to trade wool cloth and other things made in English factories for Indian products.
European products	Indian would bring furs, corn, and tobacco to these posts to trade for European products. Only friendly Indians would be good trading partner.

- Evaluating a Novel or Story
  Objective: Identify theme and plot in a fiction piece and describe the characters' actions, and events which affect the theme or plot.
- Evaluating Nonfiction
  Objective: Locate important information in an informational text and explain opinions and ideas related to this information.
- Synthesis: Put the Ideas Together
  Objective: Identify and evaluate ideas from fiction and nonfiction and integrate or synthesize ideas across texts.

Strategy Study: Visualizing in Fiction and Nonfiction

3.1. Focusing on Mental Images—Fiction (See Figure 10.12)

1. Purpose of the Minilesson
"It is important to visualize, or see a movie in your head, while reading. When you see, feel, and hear what is happening in the text, it makes it easier to understand what you are reading. It also helps you understand the plot or theme in a book. If you don't see pictures in your mind while reading or listening to someone read or speak, you may not comprehend the text. Good readers and listeners see pictures in their minds when reading, while listening to the radio, or when people speak."

2. Teaching Sequence
Have students close their eyes, relax on desks, or lay down. Begin to read a literary picture book. Don't show the illustrations. Help students focus on the mental images that the first few pages of the book evoke. Then, have students discuss as a whole group what they see in their minds. Read a few more pages and have the students discuss what they visualize. After they share as a whole group two or three times, have everyone share with one partner. Students developing proficiency in English may be able to talk more easily with a partner than in the whole-group setting. At the end of the book, have a group discussion about what students saw or didn't see in their minds during the reading. Create a chart listing their ideas. Figure 10.13 shows an example of a chart with student sketches added on with sticky notes.

3.2 Focusing on Mental Images—Nonfiction

1. Purpose of the Minilesson
This lesson has the same components as visualizing in fiction; however, it is important for students to understand how visualizing nonfiction helps them determine importance in text and connect ideas together.

"When you see, feel, and hear what is happening in the text, it makes it easier to understand what you are reading. It also helps you understand

LANGUAGE WORKSHOP

Strategy Study: Visualizing in Fiction and Nonfiction

Charts and Graphics to Aid Language Development	Lesson Choices	Teaching Focus	Books and Resources
Visualizing chart Triple T-chart with the following headings: "Phrase in Text," "I Imagined," "I Thought"	Focusing on Mental Images—Fiction Focusing on Mental Images—Nonfiction Noticing Sensory Images How Visualization Helps Us Understand Text Sketch and Compare Sketch to Show Emotions Powerful Pictures from Words Trying on a Character	Discuss images from reading with a partner. Explain and seek information from partner for a clear understanding of the other student's mental images. Learn how to visualize while teacher reads text aloud. Discuss as whole group what students see in their minds. Develop skill of visualizing nonfiction to determine importance in text and connect ideas together. Discuss mind pictures and how the reader understands the text because of the mind pictures. Develop skill to infer what the author thinks. Develop skill to change mind pictures as knowledge about a subject or a person is developed.	Gonzalez, Maya Christina. 2005. *Laughing Tomatoes.* MacLachlan, Patricia. 1994. *All the Places to Love.* MacLachlan, Patricia. 1998. *What You Know First.* Ringold, Faith. 1996. *Tar Beach.* Say, Allen. 2004. *Music for Alice.* Turkle, Brinton. 1985. *Do Not Open.* Williams, Vera B. 1991. *Cherries and Cherry Pits.* Yolen, Jane. 1987. *Owl Moon.* Zolotow, Charlotte. 2002. *If You Listen.*

FIGURE 10.12   Unit-of-Study Sheet: Visualizing in Fiction and Nonfiction

FIGURE 10.13   Visualizing Chart

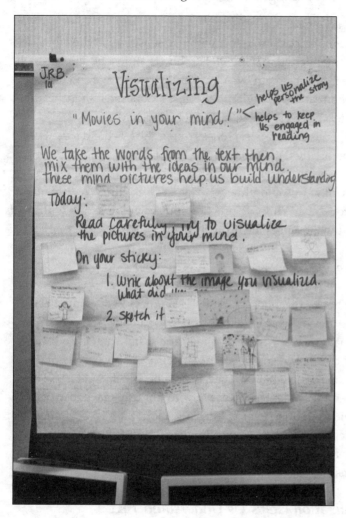

what is important in the nonfiction piece. If you can see and hear what is occurring in a nonfiction piece, it is almost like being there. You might even feel what the people feel. By visualizing the situation, you can connect to the text. You can also connect ideas with other events in our world."

2. Teaching Sequence
Students sit with a blank piece of paper on the desk or in a notebook in their laps. Begin to read from a short nonfiction text. A story from the local newspaper works well, as does a nonfiction book that is a favorite with the class. Pick a text that will have some familiarity for the students. As you read, stop and discuss as a whole group what they see in their minds. Read the remainder of the text and have the students quickly sketch what they visualize. Have the students share their sketches with a partner. Facilitate group discussion about what the students saw or didn't see in their minds during the reading. Discuss what the author did that helped them visualize a clear picture. Add their ideas to a chart titled "Visualizing Nonfiction Texts."

3.3 Noticing Sensory Images

1. Purpose of the Minilesson

"When we read it is so important to feel with our senses what the words are saying. If smoke is mentioned in the text, we should almost be able to smell the smoke; if there is an ice-cream cone melting in the sun, we should be able to taste it. Good readers feel with their senses all of the things the authors put into the text for us to smell, taste, feel, hear, and see.

"On this chart, I have written the senses down the left-hand side [prepare chart paper before lesson]. Today while I read you are going to think about what you are seeing, hearing, smelling, feeling, and tasting. Often authors use powerful words and phrases to evoke our senses. We are going to practice today together. While we practice you are going to talk with your partner about what senses the text brings out."

2. Teaching Sequence

Choose a book to model your visualization. The book or example should be different from the book you choose to read for language workshop. Poems work well because they are short. Read the poem or a page from a picture book. Describe what you see, hear, smell, feel, and taste. Then introduce the book you selected for the lesson. As you read, pause in appropriate places and have students describe what they see, hear, smell, feel, and taste. This lesson is well suited for students who are new to English. Have them discuss their ideas with a partner, even if they talk about their ideas in their first language. Then, lead a discussion in English with the whole group, encouraging students new to English to share what they feel in their minds. Write their responses on a chart.

3.4 How Visualization Helps Us Understand Text

1. Purpose of the Minilesson

"It is so important to see pictures in our head while reading. We have been talking about visualization for a few days. Today, I want you to think and share with a partner what you understand about our reading because of the mind pictures you have in your head. We don't all think alike and sometimes what is a vivid picture in my mind may not be the same picture you have in your mind. Or perhaps you will notice a different detail than I will. Think of the words that help you see something, and then tell your partner what you imagine. The words from the text don't always paint a complete picture, but what we know and learn from the text makes our mind pictures richer and more complex."

2. Teaching Sequence

After explaining the purpose of the lesson, read aloud an excerpt from any Time for Kids weekly publication or Scholastic News text. Any Time for Kids piece from the Time for Kids Nonfiction box (Teacher Created Materials 2000) also works well. These materials come on overheads as well as cardstock. The overheads serve as good examples for the minilesson and the cardstock texts work well for partner reading and discussion. After reading an example or two and discussing with the class your understanding of the text based on your mind picture, tell students, "Now we are all going to share our mind pictures and how we understand the text because of the mind pictures."

Discuss with students your thoughts as you record them on a chart. Then have the students read a section of a Time for Kids or Scholastic News text with a partner and have the students come up to the chart and record their thoughts. At the end of the workshop have students share the thinking they recorded on the chart. Have the students identify vivid details.

3.5 Sketch and Compare

1. Purpose of the Minilesson

"We are going to draw what the author makes us see or hear or feel. We might feel happy, sad, frustrated, or angry while reading. The author makes us feel these emotions by using descriptive language in his or her writing. Today we are going to notice the emotions we feel while reading. I want you to share your feelings by sketching them in your response notebook and then sharing with a partner your picture and your feelings."

2. Teaching Sequence

This is another effective lesson for students new to English. The students can express how they feel during the read-aloud by drawing a picture of their feelings or pointing to a prepared picture with a sad, happy, or neutral face. Students new to English may talk with a partner in their first language, but encourage them to share a few words with the whole group in English. They may be comfortable enough to say just a little, but encouraging them to talk in a risk-free conversation about how a book makes them feel increases language acquisition. Often the pictures in the book help them identify their feelings.

Choose a read-aloud and while reading, focus the students on how *they* feel during the reading. Do they feel angry or sad themselves? Do they feel mad at a character? Perhaps they feel comforted by the book's ending.

3.6 Sketch to Show Emotions

1. Purpose of the Minilesson

"We have been visualizing what the author makes us see or hear, but today we are going to focus on what we think the author feels. We can often glimpse the author's thoughts in an opinion piece, in powerful language, or in poetry. Inferring how the author might feel about a subject helps good readers think about the meaning of texts and how the texts connect to our lives. Today we are going to infer what the author thinks in *What You Know First*, by Patricia MacLachlan (1995).

2. Teaching Sequence

Copy page 13 from *What You Know First*. This is the page where the mother is crying because the family has to sell the farm. Show your thinking to your class. "When I read this page, the words make me feel sad and I think the author knows how this feels. I think this because the author does a very good job of making me feel sad."

Model your thinking for the students several times with other pages. You can think of this as saying to students, "When I read this _____, I felt _____. I wonder if the author had a lot of experience with _____." Read another page and have the children turn to a partner and tell their partner what they are thinking and why. Then have them speculate on the author's feelings.

3.7 Powerful Pictures from Words

This lesson is designed for more sophisticated learners or students at intermediate or advanced levels of English acquisition.

1. Purpose of Minilesson

"During the last few days we have explored how texts make us feel and how we have pictures in our heads when reading. Today, I want you to think and share with a partner how your thinking has changed because of the mind pictures you have in your head. When we read and talk and listen to others, we learn. Our mind pictures should change as we learn because we know more about a subject or a person. I want to show you how my thinking changed because of what I read. When I read *Music for Alice*, by Allen Say (2004), *my* perspective of what occurred in the Japanese interment camps during World War II deepened. Before, that moment in time was a page in a history book to me; I never felt how difficult it would be to lose everything I had because of my nationality, only to be given it back in an odd and difficult way. Today, I am going to read *Music for Alice* to you and we are going to talk about how our thinking changes as the pictures in our minds develop about Alice and her husband during the war."

2. Teaching Sequence

While reading the book, identify words and phrases that evoke powerful mind pictures. Stop and add your thinking to a triple T-chart with the following headings: "Phrase in Text," "I Imagined," and "I Thought." You should record the phrase in the text that created a powerful mind picture, a short description of the picture in your mind, and how your thinking changed or evolved.

3.8 Trying on a Character

1. Purpose of Minilesson

"Today we are going to visualize being inside a character. Why is the character doing what he's doing? What does he feel? How do we feel watching him—do we feel nervous, afraid, happy? We are going to write our ideas of what it means to be a particular character on a chart. We might think about what the character thinks and feels at the beginning, the middle, and the end of the book. We discover the character's thoughts and feelings by paying attention to how we feel while we are reading. Let me give you an example. Every time I read one of the books from The Boxcar Children series, I feel so nervous that something is going to happen to the children. Then I think about how the oldest sister feels. I think that if I were her, I would feel very brave. I want you to think like this today during our read-aloud. I want you to climb inside the skin of one of the characters and feel what he or she is feeling. This should help you enjoy the story even more.

2. Teaching Sequence

After introducing the book for the day, explain how the students will record their thoughts and ideas on a class chart. List the characters in the book you are going to read on a chart, leaving space to write student responses next to each character's name. This lesson also works well with nonfiction. You can choose a contemporary piece from Scholastic News or Time for Kids and have the students imagine feeling what the main person felt in the short news article. While reading either the fiction or nonfiction piece, stop in appropriate places and have students discuss how they think it would feel to be the character or person. Record these ideas on the chart.

Strategy Study: Clarifying Ideas in Text

4.1 Identifying Character Traits (See Figure 10.14)

1. Purpose of the Minilesson

"In order to understand what is happening in a book, it is important to understand character traits and think about how the characters' actions reveal the important ideas in the book. We are going to do this by identifying places in a book where we find the characters' actions interesting, or exciting, or difficult to understand. Then we are going to talk about what we notice and see if our talk helps us understand the ideas in the book."

2. Teaching Sequence

Begin lesson by introducing a book and showing students a character trait chart. These charts can differ depending on the grade level.

Character Trait Lesson for Kindergarten: List the names of the characters or draw a picture of the characters on the left side of the chart. Write the students' statements about each character beside the picture or name. At the end of the read-and-discuss portion of the language workshop, elicit a discussion on the students' thoughts about the book in general and record these thoughts at the top or bottom of the chart. Figure 10.15 shows an example of a character trait chart for *Mrs. Wishy-Washy* (Cowley 1999).

LANGUAGE WORKSHOP

Strategy Study: Clarifying Ideas in Text

Charts and Graphics to Aid Language Development	Lesson Choices	Teaching Focus	Books and Resources
"Get the Point" notebook entry graphic Big questions chart Paired squares chart "Character Traits" chart	Identifying Character Traits Becoming Specific in Our Character Observations Questioning to Clarify Ideas Get the Point!	Identify character traits. In order to understand what is happening in a book, it is important to understand character traits and think about how the characters' actions reveal the important ideas in the book. Develop a better understanding of the meaning of the novel, the themes, and the author's message. Provide specific examples and clear evidence to defend ideas when describing a character's traits. Understand big questions while discussing ideas around a book inquiry. Clarify ideas in the text while reading in order to understand the important ideas presented in the text. Avoid the trap of picking out the wrong facts to focus on and missing the point of the article.	Bunting, Eve. 1994. *Smokey Night.* Cowley, Joy. 1999. *Mrs. Wishy-Washy.* Dahl, Roald. 1998. *Charlie and the Chocolate Factory.* Elliot, Laura Malone. 2002. *Hunter's Best Friend at School.* Geeslin, Campbell. 2004. *Elena's Serenade.* Henkes, Kevin. 1993. *Owen.* Henkes, Kevin. 1996. *Lily's Plastic Purse.* Hobbie, Hollie. 2003. *Toot and Puddle.* "Kids Light the Way." In *Write Time for Kids Nonfiction Reading and Writing.* [Or any article from this kit.] 2000. Teacher Created Materials. Morrison, Toni. 2004. *Remember: The Journey to School Integration.* Ryan, Pam Munoz. 1999. *Riding Freedom.* Thomas, Joyce Carol. 1993. *Brown Honey in Broomwheat Tea.* Winter, Jeanette. 2005. *The Librarian of Basra: A True Story from Iraq.*

FIGURE 10.14 Unit-of-Study Sheet: Clarifying Ideas in Text

FIGURE 10.15 Character Trait Chart

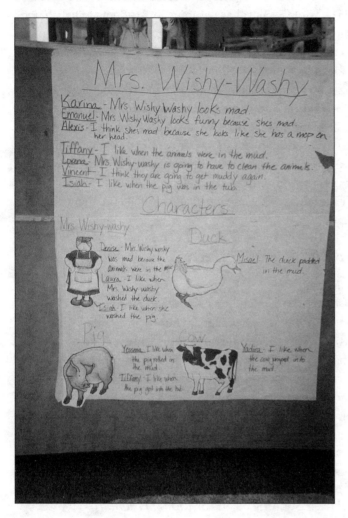

Character Trait Lesson for Primary Grades or Students New to English: Make at T-chart by listing the character names on one side of a chart and then record the students' thoughts on the opposite side of the chart. Elicit discussion during the read-aloud by stopping periodically to talk about the characters' actions and the students' perceptions about why the characters are acting in a particular way. Several books that have strong characters that young children identify with include *Owen*, by Kevin Henkes (1993), *Toot and Puddle*, by Hollie Hobbie (2003), *Lily's Plastic Purse*, by Kevin Henkes (1996b), and *Hunter's Best Friend at School*, by Laura Malone Elliot (2002).

Character Trait Lesson for Upper Grades: For older students this lesson can be taught with picture books or with a chapter book. If using a chapter book, repeat the lesson over several days. Begin the lesson by gathering students in the meeting area and showing the character trait chart (see

Appendix A). This chart is slightly different than the chart used with younger students. The triple T-chart has columns for students to list character names, character actions, and how the characters' actions affect the plot.

You can model the chart for the whole group or you can have the students record their ideas on their own copies while you model how to use the graphic organizer on a large chart. As you move through a novel, record additional thoughts about each character introduced in the chapters. You can also invite students to add ideas to their character analysis as more information surfaces in each chapter. Character personalities deepen as novels progress and often the character actions are connected to the plot and story resolution. By examining the characters, your students can develop a better understanding of the meaning of the novel, the themes, and the author's message.

4.2 Becoming Specific in Our Character Observations

1. Purpose of the Minilesson
"Lately I have noticed that we are very general when writing and reflecting about the traits and actions of the characters in our books. Today we are going to work at using specific examples and clear evidence to defend our word choices when describing a character's traits. For example, some of our responses are general, like this one [show on a chart]: 'She is nice because of her nice things.' Today while reading, I want you to write notes that are more specific about a character. When you are specific, it helps you to clar-

FIGURE 10.16   Paired Squares Chart for *Riding Freedom*

Not Clear	Clear Evidence
Sensitive to Others She's sensitive to others because she is nice.	**Sensitive to Others** Charlotte defends Hayward when William teases him about his big ears.
Hardworking I think it's because she is working hard for that guy. I think she has done a lot of hard work.	**Hardworking** At Ebenesser's ranch, Charlotte is the first one up working with the horses and the last one to bed at night.
Brave She is brave because she is doing everything.	**Brave** Charlotte runs away to find a better life even though she has nowhere to go and no one to help her.

ify the ideas in the book, and it helps you predict what might happen next based on a character's actions."

2. Teaching Sequence

After introducing the lesson, show the class a chart you have developed that lists examples of vague statements and clear statements about characters. The example in Figure 10.16 was developed for *Riding Freedom*, by Pam Munoz Ryan (1999). Use a chart with paired squares to compare ideas. A paired squares chart lists two examples about one idea in two squares that are paired together (see Appendix A).

After discussing an example of paired squares, draw a blank paired squares chart on a chart pad. Practice filling it in during the read-aloud. Choose one book suggested on the unit-of-study sheet (refer back to Figure 10.14). Remember to focus on one character. Describe the character's traits or actions with one word (on the example, Charlotte was described as sensitive, hardworking, and brave); then elicit clear statements from the group discussion and add them to the chart. Write down any statements that are unclear and discuss the difference between clear and unclear descriptions.

4.3 Questioning to Clarify Ideas

1. Purpose of the Minilesson

"During our reading we have been discussing some of the themes that we notice in the book. Well, today I want to make sure we are clear about what is happening in the book and why. I am going to pose a big question to all of you and we are going to discuss our ideas around this big question." This lesson is developed around *Charlie and the Chocolate Factory*, by Roald Dahl (1998), but any chapter book with a controversial twist is appropriate. Figure 10.17 shows an example of a chart for big questions thinking.

"It is really important to give evidence from the book to back up your statements, so you might need to check your language workshop notebooks for facts. Here's our big question for the day: Is it fair for Willy Wonka to test his inventions on the Oompa Loompas?"

2. Teaching Sequence

After introducing the question for the day, generate a list of answers that state why or why not. To generate the list, have students meet in groups of three. Have the small groups talk about their ideas about the question. Have groups jot these ideas down on sticky notes, and then reconvene as a whole group and have students share their answers. Encourage a discussion around the students' responses. Remember to take a neutral position and encourage students to participate and record their ideas on the chart paper. Students from Andrea Ermie's fourth-grade class at Lee Richmond Elementary School in Hanford, California, created the following list in response to the big question Is it fair for Willy Wonka to test his inventions on the Oompa Loompas?

FIGURE 10.17 Big Questions Chart

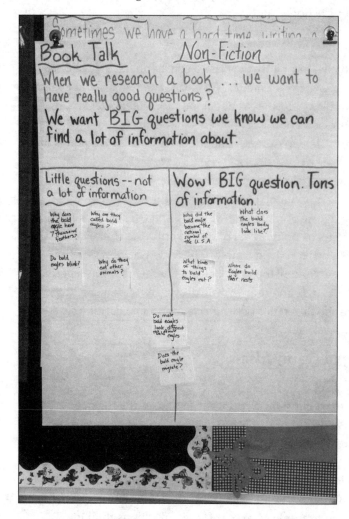

Yes, it's fair:

- If he didn't test products on them, people who bought the products in the store might be harmed.
- Oompa Loompas need to pay him back for rescuing them.
- If you test on humans, you can get in trouble or sued.
- Oompa Loompas can't get out of the factory.

No, it's not fair:

- Oompa Loompas just want to live their own lives.
- They need to be treated like anyone else.
- What if the Oompa Loompas don't want to be tested?
- When Willy Wonka brought them to the factory, he promised them a safe home, but he didn't mention testing them.

During the discussion, help students clarify their thinking by checking their response notebooks for details to back up their statements. You may need to model this several times before they understand how to clarify ideas with facts. This lesson also works well with picture books that pose deep ideas or have a controversial twist.

4.4 Get the Point!

1. Purpose of the Minilesson
"When we read nonfiction, it is important that we clarify the ideas in the text as we go along; otherwise, we might not understand the important ideas presented in the text. I've noticed that sometimes we pick out the wrong facts to focus on and we miss the point of the article. Today, we are going to focus on getting the point of whatever we are reading. Practicing how to get the point in books will also help us get the point of our conversations and the documentaries we watch when we are researching information."

2. Teaching Sequence
Choose two examples of narrative text. It works best to use short articles so the students can concentrate on getting the point without getting lost in the reading. The nonfiction cards in the Write Time for Kids Nonfiction Reading and Writing program are excellent short nonfiction texts arranged in subgroups of the nonfiction genre. The two types of nonfiction writing that work well for this lesson are narrative nonfiction and expository writing. A narrative nonfiction piece tells a story or recounts an event. Expository writing explains an idea or event or describes information. Expository writing has a different form and function than narrative nonfiction. For this lesson example I have used an expository nonfiction piece.

First, settle your class in the meeting area; make sure students are partnered in order to discuss the ideas introduced with a peer. Introduce a short article. This lesson sequence uses "Kids Light the Way" from the Write Time for Kids Nonfiction Reading and Writing program (Teacher Created Materials 2000). Read aloud the first paragraph (the "Kids Light the Way" article begins with a description of firehouse gear). Ask students to discuss the point of the first paragraph (that two kids bought thirty-five thousand dollars' worth work of gear for a local fire department). The first paragraph is usually an introduction and is a good paragraph to practice with. Some students have trouble identifying the main point in a paragraph.

Now read the next paragraph and have students discuss in pairs. The second paragraph of the article says, "The boys saw a story on the NBC TV program *Dateline* about an Oklahoma mother who raised $25,000 to buy a helmet called an IRIS (Infrared Imaging System) for her town's fire department. Its special goggles allow fire fighters to see clearly through smoke." The article goes on to explain that the woman did this because she lost her three children in a fire because the firemen couldn't see her children in the smoke. Invite your students to discuss with their partners the meaning of the next paragraph in the article you have chosen. In the article "Kids Light the Way," it would be important to make sure the students understand that the woman helped her local fire department.

Next, give paired groups one to two minutes to discuss and decide on the point of the paragraph; then have one student from each group share the group's thinking with the whole class. Continue to have students discuss the main point of each paragraph in pairs and share their ideas with the whole group.

Andrea Ermie used the "get the point" technique with her students. They read a nonfiction piece on the history of pencils and then wrote notes in their notebooks after discussing their ideas with their partners. After reading the whole article, Andrea had her students evaluate the notes; they gave themselves a star in the margin if the note was the main point or a circle if it wasn't.

APPENDIXES

Appendix A: Graphic Organizers

Appendix B: Book Lists for Units of Study

Appendix A

Graphic Organizers

Character Emotion Chart

Character Traits, Actions, and Effect on Plot

Character Trait Chart

Character Thoughts and Feelings

Paired Squares Graphic

Retelling Fiction

Retelling Nonfiction

Semantic Map—Vocabulary Web

Semantic Map—Clustering Ideas

Synopsis Sheet

Asking Questions of the Text

Wondering and Prediction Jots

Information Map

My Cubing Inquiry

Story Map

Theme Analysis

Yes/No Fact Chart

Concept Map

Text Connections

Character Emotion Chart

Name _____

Title _____

Character Name	Emotions/Feelings	Why—The Events That Cause the Characters' Feelings

Appendix A

Character Traits, Actions, and Effect on Plot

Name _____

Title _____

Character Trait	Character Action	Effect
List trait	What did the character do?	What occurred because of the character's actions?
Name: Trait:	Page	
Name: Trait:	Page	
Name: Trait:	Page	
Name: Trait:	Page	

Graphic Organizer for Student Thinking

Name _____

Title _____

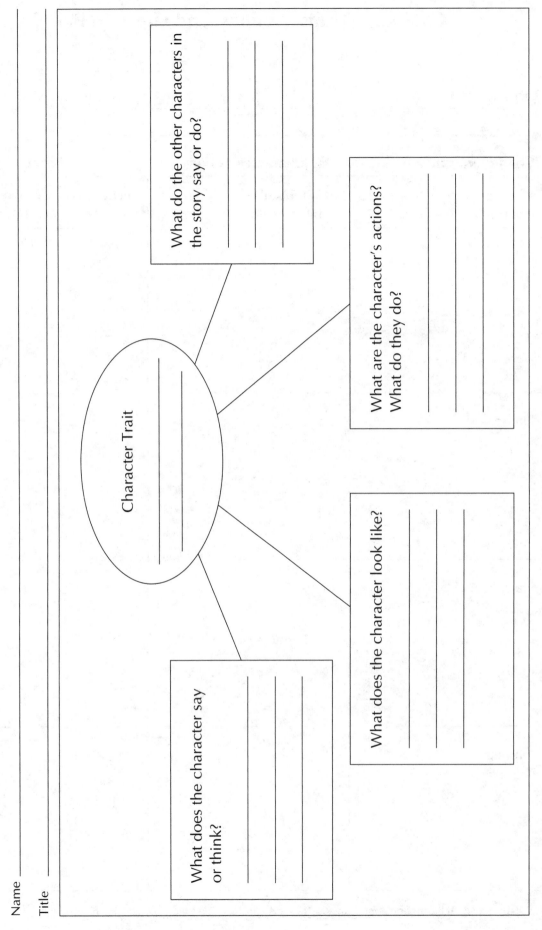

What do the other characters in the story say or do?

_____

_____

_____

What are the character's actions? What do they do?

_____

_____

_____

Character Trait

_____

_____

What does the character look like?

_____

_____

_____

What does the character say or think?

_____

_____

_____

Character Thoughts and Feelings

Name _____

Title _____

Character Thoughts and Feelings	Evidence from Text
List character thoughts/feelings.	List page number and write quote.

Paired Squares Graphic

Name _____

Title _____

Not Clear	Clear Evidence

Retelling Fiction

When good readers understand what they read, they can retell the story.

Name _____

Title:
Author:
Important Characters:
Setting or various settings:
Problem or Goal of Main Character:
Important Events:
Resolution of problem or how goal was reached:

Retelling Nonfiction

When good readers understand what they read, they can retell important facts and events.

Name _____

Title:
Author:
Topic:
Setting or various settings:
Important ideas, events, and information:
Nonfiction text features:
Author's intent:

Semantic Map—Vocabulary Web

Name _____

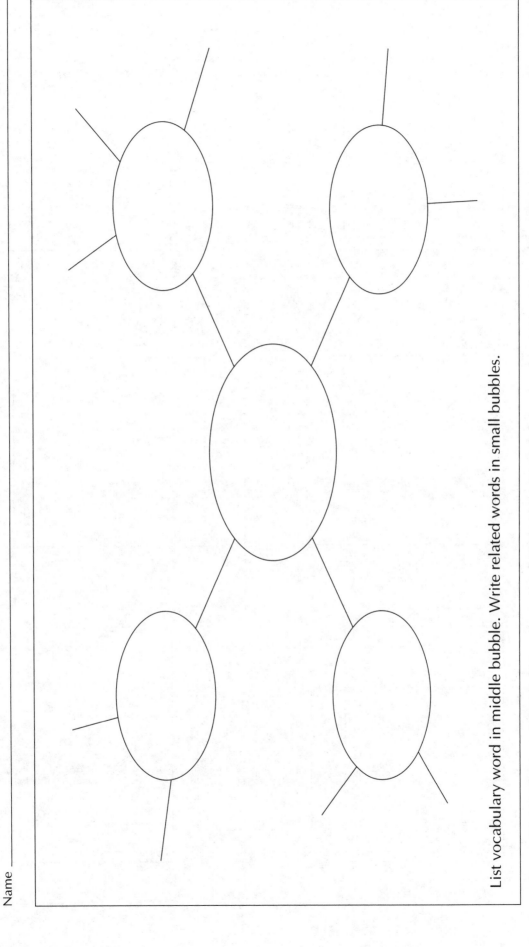

List vocabulary word in middle bubble. Write related words in small bubbles.

© 2006 by Nancy Akhavan from *Help! My Kids Don't All Speak English*. Portsmouth, NH: Heinemann.

Semantic Map—Clustering Ideas

Name _____

Topic _____

Write the main topic on the line.

Write connected ideas in the surrounding boxes.

Appendix A

Synopsis Sheet

Name _____

Title _____

Title:
Author:

Type of Text: Fantasy   Realistic Fiction   Nonfiction

What was this book mostly about?

© 2006 by Nancy Akhavan from *Help! My Kids Don't All Speak English*. Portsmouth, NH: Heinemann.

Asking Questions of the Text

Name _____

Title _____

Thin Questions	Thick Questions
The answers are *right there* in the text.	You have to think and make an inference to find the answer.

Wondering and Prediction Jots

JOT	JOT	JOT
Name _____	Name _____	Name _____
Title _____	Title _____	Title _____
Page: Wondering: Prediction:	Page: Wondering: Prediction:	Page: Wondering: Prediction:
Page: Wondering: Prediction:	Page: Wondering: Prediction:	Page: Wondering: Prediction:
Page: Wondering: Prediction:	Page: Wondering: Prediction:	Page: Wondering: Prediction:

Information Map

Title:		
Author:		
Topic:		

Important Events/ Information: 1.	2.	3.
4.	5.	6.
New Learning:		

My Cubing Inquiry

Name _____

Topic _____

State your ideas in jots!

Describe	Compare	Associate	Analyze	Apply	Argue

Story Map

Name _____

Title	
Characters	
Setting	

Events

1.

2.

3.

4.

5.

Problem	**Solution**

Theme Analysis

Name _____

Title _____

Theme	Evidence from Text
Describe theme.	List page number and write quote.

© 2006 by Nancy Akhavan from *Help! My Kids Don't All Speak English.* Portsmouth, NH: Heinemann.

Yes/No Fact Chart

Name _____

Problem Posed _____

Yes (Explain Your Thinking and Provide Facts)	**No** (Explain Your Thinking and Provide Facts)

Post a problem or idea. On the Yes side they explain their idea with facts in support of an issue; on the No side they explain and provide facts against an issue.

Concept Map

Name _____

Category	How People Felt or Thought	What Happened to These People?

Text Connections

Name _____

Book Title _____ Author _____

Page Number	**Connection** (Describe what happened in the text that you connected with)	**My Thinking** (Describe why you have this connection)

Appendix B

Book Lists for Units of Study

Books with Cultural Viewpoints

Aliki. 1998. *Marianthe's Story: Painted Words, Spoken Memories.*

Alvarez, Julia. 2000. *The Secret Footprints.*

Best, Cari. 1999. *Three Cheers for Catherine the Great.*

Bunting, Eve. 1994. *Smokey Night.*

———. 1996. *Going Home.*

———. 1997. *A Day's Work.*

Choi, Yangsook. 2001. *The Name Jar.*

Geeslin, Campbell. 2004. *Elena's Serenade.*

Grifalconi, Ann. 2002. *The Village That Vanished.*

Heide, Florence Perry, and Judith Heide Gilliland. 1992. *Sami and the Time of the Troubles.*

Joose, Barbara M. 2001. *Ghost Wings.*

Laird, Elizabeth. 1991. *Kiss the Dust.*

Look, Lenore. 1999. *Love as Strong as Ginger.*

Monk, Isabell. 1998. *Hope.*

Nye, Naomi Shihab. 1997. *Sitti's Secrets.*

On Louie, Therese. 2002. *Raymond's Perfect Present.*

Oughton, Jerrie. 1992. *How the Stars Fell into the Sky.*

Parry, Florence H. 1995. *The Day of Ahmed's Secret.*

Partridge, Elizabeth. 2001. *Oranges on Golden Mountain.*

Perez, Amada Irma. 2000. *My Very Own Room/Mi Propio Cuartito.*

Recorvitis, Helen. 2003. *My Name Is Yoon.*

Ryan, Pam Munoz. 2001. *Mice and Beans.*

Say, Allen. 1991. *Tree of Cranes.*

Soto, Gary. 1993. *Too Many Tamales.*

———. 1998. *Snapshots from the Wedding.*

Torres, Leyla. 1998. *Liliana's Grandmother.*

Winter, Jeanette. 2004. *Elsina's Clouds.*

Yoo, Paula. 2005. *Sixteen Years in Sixteen Seconds: The Sammy Lee Story.*

Novels

Armstrong, Nancy M. 1994. *Navajo Long Walk.*

Johnston, Tony. 2001. *Any Small Goodness.*

Park, Linda Sue. 2001. *A Single Shard.*

———. 2005. *Project Mulberry.*

Memoir

Abells, Chana Byers. 1986. *The Children We Remember.*

Greenfield, Eloise. 1992. *Childtimes: A Three Generation Memoir.*

Jiang, Ji Li. 1997. *Red Scarf Girl: A Memoir of the Cultural Revolution.*

Mah, Adeline Yen. 1991. *Chinese Cinderella: The True Story of an Unwanted Daughter.*

Polacco, Patricia. 1993. *The Bee Tree.*

Rylant, Cynthia. 1985. *When I Was Young in the Mountains.*

Say, Allen. 1999. *Tea with Milk.*

Ya, Chun. 2005. *Little Green: Growing Up During the Chinese Cultural Revolution.*

Books on Family and Belonging

Christensen, Bonnie. 2003. *In My Grandmother's House.*

Fleming, Virginia. 1993. *Be Good to Eddie Lee.*

Flournoy, Valerie. 1985. *The Patchwork Quilt.*

Garland, Sherry. 1997. *The Lotus Seed.*

Glenn, Sharlee. 2004. *Keeping Up with Roo.*

Houston, Gloria. 1992. *My Great-Aunt Arizona.*

Howard, Elizabeth Fitzgerald. 1991. *Aunt Flossie's Hats (and Crab Cakes Later).*

———. 1996. *What's in Aunt Mary's Room?*

Kasza, Keiko. 1996. *A Mother for Choco.*

Lester, Helen. 2003. *Something Might Happen.*

Lewis, Rose A. 2000. *I Love You Like Crazy Cakes.*

Lo, Ginnie. 2005. *Mahjong All Day Long.*

Mauner, Claudia, and Elisa Smalley. 2003. *Zoe Sophia's Scrapbook: An Adventure in Venice.*

McClintock, Barabara. 2002. *Dahlia.*

Monk, Isabell. 2001. *Family.*

Moss, Marissa. 2000. *Amelia's Family Ties.*

Muth, Jon J. 2005. *Zen Shorts.*

Ringgold, Faith. 1991. *Tar Beach.*

———. 1996. *Dinner at Aunt Connie's House.*

Rylant, Cynthia. 1987. *Silver Packages: An Appalachian Christmas Story.*

———. 2002. *The Ticky Tacky Doll.*

Stewart, Sarah. 1997. *The Gardener.*

———. 2004. *The Friend.*

Wells, Rosemary. 2003. *The Small World of Binky Braverman.*

Novels

Cameron, Ann. 2004. *Colibri.*

DiCamillo, Kate. 2000. *Because of Winn-Dixie.*

Giff, Patricia Reilly. 1999. *Lily's Crossing.*

Henkes, Kevin. 2003. *Olive's Ocean.*

Look, Lenore. 2004. *Ruby Lu, Brave and True.*

Ryan, Pam Munoz. 2004. *Becoming Naomi Leon.*

White, Ruth. 1996. *Belle Prater's Boy.*

———. 2000. *Memories of Summer.*

———. 2005. *The Search for Belle Prater.*

Books on Problem Solving, Resiliency, and Change

Bunting, Eve. 1992. *The Wall*.

———. 1993. *Fly Away Home*.

Buzzeo, Toni. 2002. *The Sea Chest*.

Cannon, Janell. 2004. *Pinduli*.

Coleman, Evelyn. 1996. *White Socks Only*.

Fleischman, Paul. 1999. *Weslandia*.

Fowler, Susi Gregg. 1998. *Circle of Thanks*.

Harvey, Amanda. 2002. *Dog Eared*.

Henkes, Kevin. 1993. *Owen*.

———. 1996a. *Chrysanthemum*.

———. 1996b. *Sheila Rae, the Brave*.

Johnson, Angela. 1998. *Gone from Home: Short Takes*.

———. 2005. *The Sweet Smell of Roses*.

Kessler, Liz. 2004. *The Tail of Emily Windsnap*.

Muth, Jon. 2002. *The Three Questions*.

Numeroff, Laura. 1999. *The Chicken Sisters*.

Polacco, Patricia. 1990a. *Just Plain Fancy*.

———. 1990b. *Thunder Cake*.

Popov, Nikolai. 1996. *Why*.

Rosenberg, Liz. 1997. *The Silence in the Mountains*.

Rylant, Cynthia. 1996. *An Angel for Solomon Singer*.

Seuss, Dr. 1984. *The Butter Battle Book*.

Waber, Bernard. 2002. *Courage*.

Weatherford, Carole Boston. 2004. *Freedom on the Menu: The Greensborough Sit-Ins*.

Wilson, Sarah. 2003a. *Big Day on the River*.

———. 2003b. *Old Turtle and the Broken Truth*.

Woodson, Jacqueline. 2002a. *Our Gracie Aunt*.

———. 2002b. *Visiting Day*.

———. 2004. *Coming on Home Soon*.

Novels

Byalick, Marcia. 2002. *Quit It.*

Creech, Sharon. 2003. *Granny Torrelli Makes Soup.*

Curtis, Christopher Paul. 1995. *The Watsons Go to Birmingham, 1963.*

Curtis, Paul. 1999. *Bud, Not Buddy.*

DiCamillo, Kate. 2003. *The Tale of Despereaux.*

Gantos, Paul. 2000. *Joey Pigza Swallows the Key.*

Giff, Patricia Reilly. 2004. *Pictures of Hollis Woods.*

Henkes, Kevin. 1998. *Sun and Spoon.*

Hesse, Karen. 1999. *Out of the Dust.*

Johnson, Angela. 2003. *A Cool Moonlight.*

Khan, Rukhsana. 2003. *Ruler of the Courtyard.*

Lasky, Kathryn. 2003a. *My America: Hope in My Heart, Sophia's Ellis Island Diary, Book One.*

————. 2003b. *My America: Hope in My Heart, Sophia's Ellis Island Diary, Book Two.*

London, Jack. 1990. *The Call of the Wild.*

Lowry, Lois. 2002. *Gooney Bird Greene.*

O'Dell, Scott. 1987. *Island of the Blue Dolphins.*

Paterson, Katherine. 1977. *The Bridge to Terabithia.*

Ryan, Pam Munoz. 2002. *Esperanza Rising.*

Rylant, Cynthia. 1993. *Missing May.*

Sachar, Louis. 2000. *Holes.*

Spinelli, Jerry. 1999. *Maniac MacGee.*

Weeks, Sarah. 2004. *So B. It.*

Books with Sensory Detail and Imagery

Carlstorm, Nancy White. 2002. *Before You Were Born.* (spiritual theme)

Creech, Sharon. 2000. *Fishing in the Air.*

DeTerlizzi, Tony. 2002. *The Spider and the Fly.*

Duncan, Lois. 2000. *I Walk at Night.*

Hest, Amy. 2004. *Mr. George Baker.*

Jeffers, Susan. 2003. *My Pony.*

LaMarche, Jim. 2000. *The Raft*.

Lawson, Julie. 1999. *Bear on the Train*.

Marten, Jacqueline Briggs. 2002. *On Sand Island*.

Pilkey, Dav. 1996. *The Paperboy*.

Rylant, Cynthia. 1996. *The Old Woman Who Named Things*.

Spinelli, Eileen. 2001. *Sophie's Masterpiece*.

Tavares, Matt. 2000. *Zachary's Ball*.

Wood, Audrey. 1984. *The Napping House*.

Yolen, Jane. 1987. *Owl Moon*.

Zolotow, Charlotte. 2002. *If You Listen*.

Books with Simple Language for Young Children and Students New to English

Aston, Diana Hutts. 2004. *Bless This Mouse*.

Boxall, Ed. 2004. *Scoot on Top of the World*.

Bynum, Janie. 2001. *Altoona Up North*.

Cummings, Pat. 1998. *My Aunt Came Back*.

Degen, Bruce. 2000. *Daddy Is a Doodlebug*.

Edwards, Pamela Duncan. 2003. *Rosie's Roses*.

Falconer, Ian. 2000. *Olivia*.

Fleischman, Paul. 2004. *Sidewalk Circus*. (This wordless book invites discussion and vocabulary building.)

Freeman, Don. 2004. *Manuelo the Praying Mantis*.

French, Jackie. 2002. *Diary of a Wombat*.

Graham-Barber, Linda. 2004. *Spy Hops and Belly Flops*.

Gray, Nigel. 1988. *A Country Far Away*.

Guest, C. Z. 2000. *Tiny Green Thumb*.

Haan, Amanda. 2003. *I Call My Hand Gentle*.

Heap, Sue. 2004. *Four Friends in the Garden*.

Hest, Amy. 2001. *Kiss Good Night*.

———. 2003. *You Can Do It, Sam*.

Mannis, Celeste Davidson. 2002. *One Leaf Rides the Wind*.

Marshall, Rita. 1992. *I Hate to Read*.

Martin, Bill Jr. 1970. *The Turning of the Year*. (written as a list book)

Thomson, Pat. 2003. *Drat That Fat Cat!*

Wallace, John. 2003. *Anything for You*.

Weeks, Sarah. 1995. *Follow the Moon*.

———. 2002. *Oh My Gosh, Mrs. McNosh*.

Wells, Rosemary. 1997. *Bunny Cakes*.

———. 2000. *Max Cleans Up*.

Wood, Audrey. 1992. *Silly Sally*.

Beautiful Language and Repetitive Lines

Aston, Diana Hutts. 2004. *When You Were Born*.

Blos, Joan W. 1987. *Old Henry*.

Brian, Janeen. 2001. *Where Does Thursday Go?*

Brinckloe, Julie. 1986. *Fireflies*.

Chaconas, Dori. 2000. *On a Wintry Morning*.

Creech, Sharon. 2000. *Fishing in the Air*.

Fletcher, Ralph. 2003. *Hello, Harvest Moon*.

Fraustino, Lisa Rowe. 2001. *The Hickory Chair*.

Hesse, Karen. 1999. *Come on, Rain!*

Hooper, Meredith. 2000. *River Story*.

Hoose, Phillip, and Hannah Hoose. 1998. *Hey Little Ant*.

Katz, Karen. 1999. *The Colors of Us*.

Johnston, Tony. 2002. *That Summer*.

Lawler, Janet. 2003. *If Kisses Were Colors*.

Lester, Helen. 1990. *Tacky the Penguin*.

MacLachlan, Patricia. 1994. *All the Places to Love*.

Mannis, Celeste Davidson. 2002. *One Leaf Rides the Wind: Counting in a Japanese Garden*.

Meyers, Walter Dean. 1993. *Brown Angels: An Album of Pictures and Verse*.

———. 2003. *Blues Journey*.

Rylant, Cynthia. 1998. *Scarecrow*.

———. 2004. *Long Night Moon.*

Schaefer, Carole Lexa. 2001. *Sometimes Moon.*

Van Laan, Nancy. 2000. *When Winter Comes.*

Weeks, Sarah. 2003. *Without You.*

———. 2004. *If I Were a Lion.*

Wood, Douglas. 1998. *Making the World.*

Yolen, Jane. 1997. *Nocturne.*

Onomatopoeia

Buzzeo, Tony. 2004. *Little Loon and Papa.*

Cole, Babette. 2001. *Truelove.*

McDonald, Megan. 2004. *Judy Moody, M.D. The Doctor Is In!*

Rylant, Cynthia. 1991. *Night in the Country.*

Weeks, Sarah. 2004. *Paper Parade.*

Wood, Audrey. 1997. *Bird Song.*

Books Loaded with Vocabulary

Clearly, Brian P. 1999. *A Mink, a Fink, a Skating Rink: What Is a Noun?*

———. 2001. *Hairy, Scary, Ordinary: What Is an Adjective?*

———. 2003. *Dearly, Nearly, Insincerely: What Is an Adverb?*

———. 2004a. *I and You and Don't Forget Who: What Is a Pronoun?*

———. 2004b. *Pitch and Throw, Grasp and Know: What Is a Synonym?*

Gaiman, Neil. 2003. *The Wolves in the Walls.*

Hopkins, Lee Bennett. 2004. *Wonderful Words: Poems About Reading, Writing, Listening and Speaking.*

Jones, Charlotte Foltz. 1999. *Eat Your Words: A Fascinating Look at the Language of Food.*

Lewis, J. Patrick. 2001. *A Burst of Firsts: Doers, Shakers, and Record Breakers.*

McHenry, E. B. 2004. *Poodlena.*

Merriam, Eve. 1985. *Blackberry Dance.*

Perkins, Lynne Rae. 2003. *Snow Music.*

Schertle, Alice. 2003. *When the Moon Is High.*

Whybrow, Ian. 2001. *Wish, Change, Friend.*

Willard, Nancy. 2003. *The Mouse, the Cat and Grandmother's Hat.*

Williams, Kit. 1979. *Masquerade.*

Poetry

Attenborough, Liz. 2001. *Poetry by Heart: A Child's Book of Poems to Remember.*

Brenner, Barabara. 2000. *Voices: Poetry and Art from Around the World.*

Esbensen, Barbara Juster. 1996. *Echoes for the Eye: Poems to Celebrate Patterns in Nature.*

Feelings, Tom, and Kwame Dawes. 2004. *I Saw Your Face.*

George, Kristine O'Connell. 2002. *Little Dog and Duncan.*

Heard, Georgia. 1997. *Creatures of the Earth, Sea, and Sky: Poems.*

———. 2002. *This Place I Know: Poems of Comfort.*

James, Simon. 1999. *Days Like This: A Collection of Small Poems.* (wonderful book for students new to English)

Katz, Susan. 2005. *Looking for Jaguar: And Other Rain Forest Poems.*

Lee, Dennis. 2000. *Bubblegum Delicious.*

Median, Jane. 1999. *My Name Is Jorge: On Both Sides of the River.*

Michelson, Richard. 1996. *Animals That Ought to Be: Poems About Imaginary Pets.*

Noda, Takayo. 2003. *Dear World.*

Nye, Naomi Shihab. 1998. *The Space Between Our Footsteps.*

Soto, Gary. 2002. *Fearless Fernie: Hanging Out with Fernie and Me.*

———. 2005. *Worlds Apart: Traveling with Fernie and Me.*

Steptoe, Javaka. 1997. *In Daddy's Arms I Am Tall: African Americans Celebrating Fathers.*

Thomas, Joyce Carol. 1993. *Brown Honey in Broomwheat Tea.*

Weatherford, Carole Boston. 2002. *Remember the Bridge: Poems of a People.*

Wong, Janet S. 2000. *Night Garden: Poems from the World of Dreams.*

Nonfiction Texts

Brown, Don. 2002. *Far Beyond the Garden Gate: Alexandra David-Neel's Journey to Lhasa.*

Cooper, John. 2005. *Season of Rage.*

Cowley, Joy. 2005. *Chameleon, Chameleon.*

Davis, Lucile. 1999. *Cesar Chavez.*

Goldfarb, Mace. 1982. *Fighters, Refugees, Immigrants: A Story of the Hmong.*

Hudson, Wade. 2004. *Powerful Words: More than 200 Years of Extraordinary Writing by African Americans.*

Jocelyn, Marthe. 2005. *A Home for Foundlings.*

Katz, William Loren. 1996. *Black West.*

Kent, Deborah. 1995. *Black Women of the Old West.*

———. 2004. *The Changing Face of America: Hispanic Roots, Hispanic Pride.*

King, Wilma. 2000. *Children of the Emancipation.*

Low, William. 1997. *Chinatown.*

Major, John S., and Betty J. Belanus. 2002. *Caravan to America: Living Arts of the Silk Road.*

Millett, Sandra. 2002. *First Peoples: The Hmong of South Asia.*

Myers, Walter Dean. 1995. *One More River to Cross: An African American Photograph Album.*

Nelson, Marilyn. 2001. *Carver: A Life in Poems.*

Roman, Michelle. 2001. *Becoming Cesar Chavez.*

Rubin, Susan Goldman. 2000. *Fireflies in the Dark: The Story of Friedl Dicker-Brandeis and the Children of Terezin.*

Shulevitz, Uri. 2005. *The Travels of Benjamin of Tudela: Through Three Continents in the Twelfth Century.*

Sis, Peter. 2001. *A Small Tale from the Far, Far North.*

Stanley, Jerry. 1994. *I Am an American.*

Stearman, Kaye. 2001. *Homeless: Why Do People Live on the Streets?*

Unicef. 1994. *I Dream of Peace: Images of War by Children of Former Yugoslavia.*

Yin. 2001. *Coolies.*

Books on Rights

Bridges, Ruby. 1999. *Through My Eyes.*

Freedman, Russell. 2004. *The Voice That Challenged a Nation: Marion Anderson and the Struggle for Equal Rights.*

Hopkinson, Deborah. 1995. *Sweet Clara and the Freedom Quilt.*

Johnson, Angela. 2003. *I Dream of Trains.*

Krull, Kathleen. 2003. *Harvesting Hope: The Story of Cesar Chavez.*

Levine, Ellen. 2000. *Freedom's Children: Young Civil Rights Activists Tell Their Own Stories.*

Lowry, Lois. 1998. *Number the Stars.*

Morrison, Toni. 2004. *Remember: The Journey to School Integration.*

Polacco, Patricia. 1994. *Pink and Say.*

———. 2000. *The Butterfly.*

Ringgold, Faith. 1995. *Aunt Harriet's Underground Railroad in the Sky.*

Stamaty, Mark Alan. 2004. *Alia's Mission: Saving the Books of Iraq.*

Turk, Mary. 2000. *The Civil Rights Movement for Kids: A History with 21 Activities.*

Winter, Jeanette. 2005. *The Librarian of Basra: A True Story from Iraq.*

Children's Literature References

Ada, Alma Flor. 1995. *My Name Is Maria Isabel*. New York: Aladdin.

Aliki, 1998. *Marianthe's Story: Painted Words, Spoken Memories*. New York: Greenwillow.

Barron, T. A. 2004. *High as a Hawk: A Brave Girl's Historic Climb*. New York: Philomel.

Beach, Judi K. 2003. *Names for Snow*. New York: Hyperion Books for Children.

Bridges, Ruby. 1999. *Through My Eyes*. New York: Scholastic.

Bunting, Eve. 1998. *So Far from the Sea*. New York: Clarion.

Cohen, Barbara. 1998. *Molly's Pilgrim*. New York: Harper Trophy.

Cowley, Joy. 1999. *Mrs. Wishy-Washy*. New York: Philomel.

Dahl, Roald. 1998. *Charlie and the Chocolate Factory*. New York: Puffin.

Davidson, Margaret. 1995. *Helen Keller: A Scholastic Biography*. New York: Scholastic.

Davis, Lucile. 1997. *Cesar Chavez*. Mankato, MN: Bridgestone.

dePaola, Tomie. 1988. *The Mysterious Giant of Barletta*. New York: Voyager.

Donovan, Sandra. 2004. *Rosa Parks: An African American Biography*. Oxford, England: Raintree.

Elliot, Laura Malone. 2002. *Hunter's Best Friend at School*. New York: Harper Collins.

Fowler, Susi Gregg. 1998. *Circle of Thanks*. New York: Scholastic.

Gandos, Paul. 2001. *Joey Pigza Swallowed the Key*. New York: Harper Trophy.

Grant, James P. 1994. *I Dream of Peace: Images of War by Children of Former Yugoslavia*. New York: HarperCollins.

Henkes, Kevin. 1988. *Chester's Way*. New York: Greenwillow.

———. 1993. *Owen*. New York: Greenwillow.

———. 1996a. *Chrysanthemum*. New York: HarperTrophy.

———. 1996b. *Lily's Plastic Purse*. New York: Greenwillow.

Hobbie, Hollie. 2003. *Toot and Puddle: Charming Opal*. New York: Little, Brown.

Jenkins, Emily. 2004. *My Favorite Thing (According to Alberta)*. New York: Anne Schwartz.

Lawler, Janet. 2003. *If Kisses Were Colors*. New York: Dial.

Lovell, Patty. 2001. *Molly Lou Melon*. New York: G. P. Putnam's Sons.

MacLachlan, Patricia. 1995. *What You Know First*. New York: Joanna Cotler.

Morrison, Toni with Slade Morrison. 2002. *The Big Box*. New York: Hyperion/Jump at the Sun.

Munson, Derek. 2000. *Enemy Pie*. San Francisco: Chronicle.

Numeroff, Laura. 2004. *Beatrice Doesn't Want To*. New York: Candlewick.

O'Neill, Alexis. 2002. *The Recess Queen*. New York: Scholastic.

Parr, Todd. 2004. *The Peace Book*. New York: Megan Tingley.

Ryan, Pam Muñoz. 1999. *Riding Freedom*. New York: Scholastic.

———. 2002. *Esperanza Rising*. New York: Scholastic.

———. 2004. *Becoming Naomi Leon*. New York: Scholastic.

San Souci, Robert D. 1997. *Two Bear Cubs: A Miwok Legend from California's Yosemite Valley*. Yosemite National Park, CA: Yosemite Association.

———. 2002. *The Silver Charm*. New York: Doubleday.

Say, Allen. 2000. *The Sign Painter*. Boston: Houghton Mifflin.

———. 2004. *Music for Alice*. Boston: Houghton Mifflin.

Scholes, Katharine. 1994. *Peace Begins with You*. New York: Little, Brown.

Soto, Gary. 1993. *Too Many Tamales*. New York: G. P. Putnam's Sons.

———. 2003. *Cesar Chavez: A Hero for Everyone*. New York: Aladdin.

Teacher Created Materials. 2000. *Write Time for Kids: A Non-fiction Reading and Writing Program*. Westminister, CA: Teacher Created Materials.

Turner, Ann. 1995. *Nettie's Trip South*. New York: Aladdin.

Ward, Helen. 2001. *The Tin Forest*. New York: Dutton Children's.

Weiss, George David. 1995. *What a Wonderful World*. New York: Atheneum.

Whitcomb, Mary E. 1998. *Odd Velvet*. San Francisco: Chronicle.

Whitehouse, P. 2003. *Tiger*. Chicago: Reed Educational and Professional.

Woodson, Jacqueline. 2001. *The Other Side*. New York: G. P. Putnam's Sons.

References

Akhavan, Nancy. 2004. *How to Align Literacy Instruction, Assessment, and Standards: And Achieve Results You NEVER Dreamed Possible.* Portsmouth, NH: Heinemann.

Allington, Richard L., and Patricia M. Cunningham. 2001. *Schools That Work: Where All Children Read and Write.* 2d ed. New York: Allyn and Bacon.

Anderson, Billie V., and John G. Barnitz. 1998. "Cross-Cultural Schemata and Reading Comprehension Instruction." In *Literacy Instruction for Culturally and Linguistically Diverse Students,* ed. Michael F. Optiz, 95–101. Newark, DE: International Reading Association.

Anderson, R. C., and P. D. Pearson. 1984. "A Schematic-Theoretic View of Basic Processes in Reading." In *Handbook of Reading Research,* ed. P. D. Pearson, 255–91. White Plains, NY: Longman.

Anderson, R. C., P. T. Wilson, and L. G. Fielding. 1998. "Growth in Reading and How Children Spend Their Time Outside of School." *Reading Research Quarterly* 23: 285–303.

Armbuster, B., F. Lehr, and J. Osborn. 2001. *Put Reading First: The Research Building Blocks for Teaching Children to Read.* Jessup, MD: National Institute for Literacy.

Avalos, M. A. 2003. "Effective Second–Language Reading Transition: From Learner-Specific to Generic Instructional Models." *Bilingual Research Journal* 27 (2): 171–99.

Barnitz, John G. 1998. "Discourse Diversity: Principles for Authentic Talk and Literacy Instruction." In *Literacy Instruction for Culturally and Linguistically Diverse Students,* ed. Michael F. Optiz, 64–70. Newark, DE: International Reading Association.

Barton, Paul E. 2004. "Why Does the Gap Persist?" *Educational Leadership* 62 (3): 9–13.

Beaver, Joetta. 2004. *Developmental Reading Assessment*. Parsippany, NJ: Pearson Education.

Beck, Isabel, Margaret G. McKeown, and Linda Kucan. 2002. *Bringing Words to Life: Robust Vocabulary Instruction*. New York: Guilford.

Biemiller, Andrew. 1999. *Language and Reading Success*. Brookline, MA: Brookline.

———. 2001. "Teaching Vocabulary: Early, Direct, and Sequential." *American Educator* (Spring). www.aft.org/pubs-reports/american_educator/ spring2001/vocab.html. Accessed March 7, 2005.

Block, C. C., and M. Pressley, eds. 2002. *Comprehension Instruction: Research-Based Best Practices*. New York: Guilford.

Calkins, L. 2001. *The Art of Teaching Reading*. New York: Addison Wesley.

Carlo, María, Diane August, Barry McLaughlin, Catherine E. Snow, Cheryl Dressler, David N. Lippman, Teresea J. Lively, and Claire E. White. 2004. "Closing the Gap: Addressing the Vocabulary Needs of English-Language Learners in Bilingual and Mainstream Classrooms." *Reading Research Quarterly* 39 (2): 188–215.

Cazden, C. 2001. *Classroom Discourse: The Language of Teaching and Learning*. Portsmouth, NH: Heinemann.

Chall, Jeanne S., and Vicki A. Jacobs. 1996. "The Reading, Writing, and Language Connection." In *Literacy and Education: Essays in Memory of Dina Feitelson*, ed. J. Shimron, 33–48. Cresskill, NJ: Hampton.

———. 2003. "The Classic Study on Poor Children's Fourth-Grade Slump." *American Educator* 27 (1): 13–14.

Chamot, Anna Uhl, and J. Michael O'Malley. 1993. *The CALLA Handbook: Implementing the Cognitive Academic Language Learning Approach*. New York: Addison Wesley.

———. 1994. "Instructional Approaches and Teaching Procedures." In *Kids Come in All Languages: Reading Instruction for ESL Students*, ed. Karen Spangenber-Urbshat and Robert Pritchard, 82–107. Newark, DE: International Reading Association.

Christian, Donna. 1997. "Vernacular Dialects in U.S. Schools." *ERIC Language and Linguistics Digest*. Washington, DC: Office of Educational Research and Improvement, U.S. Department of Education.

Crandall, Joann. 1994. "Content-Centered Language Learning." *ERIC Digest*. Washington, DC: ERIC Clearinghouse on Languages and Linguistics.

Crawford, Alan N. 2003. "Communicative Approaches to Second-Language Acquisition: The Bridge to Second-Language Literacy." In *English Learners: Reaching the Highest Level of English Literacy*, ed. Gilbert G. Garcia, 125–49. Newark, DE: International Reading Association.

Cummins, Jim. 1989. *Empowering Minority Students*. Sacramento, CA: California Association for Bilingual Education.

———. 1991. *Empowering Culturally and Linguistically Diverse Students with Learning Problems.* ERIC EC Digest no. E500. Arlington, VA: ERIC Clearinghouse on Disabilities and Gifted Education.

———. 2003. "Reading and the Bilingual Student: Fact and Friction." In *English Learners: Reaching the Highest Level of English Literacy*, ed. Gilbert G. Garcia, 2–33. Newark, DE: International Reading Association.

Cunningham, Anne E., and Keith E. Stanovich. 1998. "What Reading Does for the Mind." *American Educator* (Spring/Summer): 1–8.

Daniels, Harvey, and Steven Zemelman. 2003. "Out with Textbooks, in with Learning." *Educational Leadership* 61 (4): 36–40.

Darling-Hammond, L. 1997. *The Right to Learn: A Blueprint for Creating Schools That Work.* San Francisco: Jossey-Bass.

Davis, Patricia H. 1991. *Cognition and Learning: A Review of the Literature with References to Ethnolinguistic Minorities.* Dallas: Summer Institute of Linguistics.

Delpit, Lisa. 1989. *Other People's Children: Cultural Conflict in the Classroom.* New York: New.

Delpit, Lisa, and Joanne Kilgour Dowdy, eds. 2002. *The Skin That We Speak: Thoughts on Language and Culture in the Classroom.* New York: New.

Dutro, Susana, and Carrol Moran. 2003. "Rethinking English Language Instruction: An Architectural Approach." In *English Learners: Reaching the Highest Level of English Literacy*, ed. Gilbert G. Garcia, 227–58. Newark, DE: International Reading Association.

Echevarria, Jana, and Anne Graves. 2002. *Sheltered Content Instruction: Teaching English-Language Learners with Diverse Abilities.* New York: Allyn and Bacon.

Fountas, Irene C., and Gay Su Pinnell. 1996. *Guided Reading: Good First Teaching for All Children.* Portsmouth, NH: Heinemann.

———. 2005. *The Fountas and Pinnell Leveled Book List, K–8, 2006 Edition.* Portsmouth, NH: Heinemann.

Franklin, John. 2004. "Louder Than Words: How K–12 World Language Teachers Are Meeting New Challenges." *Curriculum Update* (Fall). 1–3, 6–8.

Freeman, David, and Yvonne Freeman. 1998. *ESL/EFL Teaching: Principles for Success.* Portsmouth, NH: Heinemann.

———. 2000. *Teaching Reading in Multilingual Classrooms.* Portsmouth, NH: Heinemann.

———. 2003. "Teaching English Learners to Read: Learning or Acquisition?" In *English Learners: Reaching the Highest Level of English Literacy*, ed. Gilbert G. Garcia, 34–54. Newark, DE: International Reading Association.

———. 2004. "Three Types of English Language Learners." *School Talk* 9 (4): 1–3.

Garan, Elaine M. 2004. *In Defense of Our Children*. Portsmouth, NH: Heinemann.

Garcia, Gilbert G. 2003. Preface. In *English Learners: Reaching the Highest Levels of English Literacy*, ed. Gilbert G. Garcia, ix–xi. Newark, DE: International Reading Association.

Genesee, Fred. 1994. *Integrating Language and Content: Lessons from Immersion*. Educational Practice Report (11). National Center for Research on Cultural Diversity and Second Language Learning. Washington, DC: Center for Applied Linguistics.

Goldenberg, Claude. 2001. "Learning to Read While Learning English." *Education Week*, May 9. www.edweek.org/ew/articles/2001/05/09/34goldenberg.h20.html. Accessed March 8, 2005.

Goodman, Kenneth S. 2003. "Miscue Analsis: Theory and Reality in Reading." In *On the Revolution of Reading: The Selected Writings of Kenneth S. Goodman*, ed. Alan D. Flurkey and Jingguo Xu, 124–36. Portsmouth, NH: Heinemann.

Gutiérrez, Kris D. 2001. "What's New in the English Language Arts: Challenging Policies and Practices, ¿y qué?" *Language Arts* 78 (6): 564–69.

Hale, J. E. 2004. "How Schools Shortchange African American Children." *Educational Leadership* 62 (3): 34–38.

Haritos, Calliope. 2003. "Listening, Remembering, and Speaking in Two Languages: How Did You Do That?" *Bilingual Research Journal* 27 (1): 73–94.

Haycock, K. 2001a. "Closing the Achievement Gap." *Educational Leadership* 58 (6): 6–11.

———. 2001b. "New Frontiers for a New Century." *Thinking K–16* 5 (2): 1–2.

Helman, Lori A. 2005. "Using Literacy Assessment Results to Improve Teaching for English-Language Learners." *The Reading Teacher* 58 (7): 668–77.

Hernández, Ana. 2003. "Making Content Instruction Accessible for English Language Learners." In *English Learners: Reaching the Highest Level of English Literacy*, ed. Gilbert G. Garcia, 125–49. Newark, DE: International Reading Association.

Herrell, Adrienne, and Michael Jordan. 2004. *Fifty Strategies for Teaching English Language Learners*. 2d ed. Upper Saddle River, NJ: Pearson Education.

Herrera, S. G., and Kevin G. Murray. 2005. *Mastering ESL and Bilingual Methods: Differentiated Instruction for Culturally and Linguistically Diverse (CLD) Students*. Boston: Pearson Education.

Hindley, Joanne. *In the Company of Children*. Portland, ME: Stenhouse.

Hirsch, E. D. Jr. 2003. "Reading Comprehension Requires Knowledge of Words and the World." *American Educator* (Spring): 10–13, 16–22, 28–29.

Houghton Mifflin Company. 1998. *Spelling and Vocabulary*. Boston: Houghton Mifflin.

Jimenez, R. T., G. E. Garcia, and P. D. Pearson. 1996. "The Reading Strategies of Bilingual Latina/o Students Who Are Successful English Readers: Opportunities and Obstacles." *Reading Research Quarterly* 31 (1): 90–112.

Krashen, S. 1997. "Bridging Inequity with Books." *Educational Leadership* 55 (4): 18–2.

———. 2003. *Explorations in Language Acquisition and Use*. Portsmouth, NH: Heinemann.

Lehr, Fran, Jean Osborn, and Elfrieda H. Hiebert. 2004. "A Focus on Vocabulary." In *Pacific Resources for Education and Learning*. U.S. Department of Education Regional Educational Laboratory Program, award no. ED01C0014. Honolulu, HI: Pacific Resources for Education and Learning.

Liben, David, and Meredith Liben. 2005. "Learning to Read in Order to Learn: Building a Program for Upper-Elementary Students." *Phi Delta Kappan* 86 (5): 401–6.

Marzano, Robert. 2003. *What Works in Schools: Translating Research into Action*. Alexandria, VA: Association for Supervision and Curriculum Development.

Marzano, Robert J., Debra Pickering, and Jane E. Pollack. 2001. *Classroom Instruction That Works: Researched-Based Strategies for Increasing Student Achievement*. Alexandria, VA: Association for Supervision and Curriculum Development.

McNeil, Linda. 2000. "The Educational Costs of Standardization." *Rethinking Schools Online* 14 (2). www.rethinkingschools.org/archive/14_04/tex144.shtml. Accessed April 12, 2005.

Miramontes, Ofelia B., Adel Nadeau, and Nancy L. Commins. 1997. *Restructuring Schools for Linguistic Diversity: Linking Decision Making to Effective Programs*. New York: Teachers College Press.

Moss, Barbara. 2003. *Exploring the Literature of Fact*. New York: Guilford.

Nagy, William E. 1988. *Teaching Vocabulary to Improve Reading Comprehension*. Newark, DE: International Reading Association.

Nagy, William E., and R. C. Anderson. 1984. "How Many Words Are There in Printed English?" *Reading Research Quarterly* 19: 304–30.

Nathenson-Mejia, Sally, and Kathy Escamilla. 2003. "Connecting with Latino Children: Bridging Cultural Gaps with Children's Literature." *Bilingual Research Journal* 27 (1): 101–16.

National Institute of Child Health and Human Development (NICHHD). (2000). *Report of the National Reading Panel. Teaching Children to Read: An Evidence-Based Assessment of the Scientific Research Literature on Reading and Its Implications for Reading Instruction. NIH Publication no. 00-4769.* Washington, DC: U.S. Government Printing Office.

New Standards Speaking and Listening Committee. 2001. *Speaking & Listening for Preschool Through Third Grade.* Pittsburgh: National Center on Education and the Economy.

Olsen, L., and A. Jaramillo. 1999. *Turning the Tides of Exclusion: A Guide for Educators and Advocates for Immigrant Students.* Oakland, CA: California Tomorrow.

Owocki, Gretchen. 2003. *Comprehension: Strategic Instruction for K–3 Students.* Portsmouth, NH: Heinemann.

Owocki, Gretchen, and Yetta M. Goodman. 2002. *Kidwatching: Documenting Children's Literacy Development.* Portsmouth, NH: Heinemann.

Pearson, P. David, and Nell K. Duke. 2002. "Comprehension Instruction in the Primary Grades." In *Comprehension Instruction: Researched-Based Best Practices,* ed. Cathy Collins Block and Michael Pressley, 247–58. New York: Guilford.

Peregoy, Suzanne, F. and Owen F. Boyle. 1997. *Reading, Writing, and Learning in ESL: A Resource Book for K–12 Teachers.* 2d ed. New York: Longman.

Pressley, Michael. 2002. *Reading Instruction That Works: The Case for Balanced Teaching.* 2d ed. New York: Guilford.

Pressley, Michael, and Cathy Collins Block. 2002. "Summing Up: What Comprehension Instruction Could Be." In *Comprehension Instruction: Researched-Based Best Practices,* ed. Cathy Collins Block and Michael Pressley, 383–92. New York: Guilford.

Ramirez, J. David, Sandra D. Yuen, and Dena R. Ramey. 1991. *Final Report Structured English Immersion Strategy, Early-Exit and Late-Exit Transitional Bilingual Education Programs for Language Minority Students.* San Mateo, CA: Aguirre International.

Richek, Margaret Ann. 2005. "Words Are Wonderful: Interactive, Time-Efficient Strategies to Teach Meaningful Vocabulary." *The Reading Teacher* 58 (5): 414–23.

Rigg, P., and V. G. Allen. 1989. *When They Don't All Speak English: Integrating the ESL Student into the Regular Classroom.* Urbana, IL: National Council of Teachers of English.

Robb, Laura, Ron Klemp, and Wendell Schwartz. 2002. *Readers Handbook: A Student Guide for Reading and Learning.* Wilmington, MA: Great Source.

Rothstein-Fisch, Carrie, Patricia M. Greenfield, and Elise Trumbull. 1999. "Bridging Cultures with Classroom Strategies." *Educational Leadership* 56 (7): 64–67.

Ruiz-de-Velasco, Jorge, Michael E. Fix, and Beatriz Chu Clewell. 2000. *Overlooked and Underserved: Immigrant Students in U.S. Secondary Schools.* Research report. Urban Institute. www.urban.org/urlprint.cfm?ID=7048. Accessed December 28, 2004.

Rumberger, Russell W., and Brenda Arellano Anguiano. 2004. *Understanding and Addressing the California Latino Achievement Gap in Early Elementary School.* Riverside, CA: University of California Latino Policy Institute.

Scarcella, Robin. 2003. *Academic English: A Conceptual Framework.* The University of California Linguistic Minority Research Institute Technical Report 2003-1. Irvine, CA: University of California Linguistic Minority Research Institute.

Shefelbine, John. 2004. Developing English Learner Vocabulary Through Content Subject Matter Teaching. California Reading Association Convention, November 2, 2004. San Jose, CA.

Shin, Hyon B., with Rosalind Brun. 2003. "Language Use and English Speaking Ability: 2000." *Census 2000 Brief.* www.census.gov/prod/2003pubs/c2kbr-29.pdf. Accessed March 8, 2005.

Short, Deborah, and Jana Echevarría. 2004. "Teacher Skills to Support English Language Learners." *Educational Leadership* 62 (4): 8–13.

Short, Kathy G., Jerome C. Harste, and Carolyn Burke. 1996. *Creating Classrooms for Authors and Inquirers.* 2d ed. Portsmouth, NH: Heinemann.

Snow, M. A., M. Met, and F. Genesee. 1989. "A Conceptual Framework for the Integration of Language and Content in Second/Foreign Language Instruction." *TESOL Quarterly* 23: 201–17.

Stahl, Steven A. 1998. *Vocabulary Development.* Brookline, MA: Brookline.

———. 2003. "How Words Are Learned Incrementally Over Time." *American Educator* (Spring): 18–19.

Stahl, Steven A., and William E. Nagy. In press. *Teaching Word Meanings.* Mahwah, NJ: Lawrence Erlbaum.

Taylor, E. 1999. "Bring in 'Da Noise': Race, Sports, and the Role of Schools." *Educational Leadership* 56 (7): 75–78.

Teachers of English to Speakers of Other Languages, Inc. (TESOL). 1997. *ESL Standards for Pre-K–12 Students.*

Thomas, Wayne P., and Virginia Collier. 1997a. *School Effectiveness for Language Minority Students.* NCBE Resource Collection series no. 9. Washington, DC: National Clearinghouse for Bilingual Education.

———. 1997b. "Two Languages Are Better Than One." *Educational Leadership* 55 (4): 23–26.

———. 1999. "Accelerated Schooling for English Language Learners." *Educational Leadership* 56 (7): 47–49.

Tompkins, Gail E. 1997. *Literacy for the 21st Century: A Balanced Approach.* Upper Saddle River, NJ: Prentice-Hall.

Torgesen, Joseph K. 2004. "Preventing Early Reading Failure and Its Devastating Downward Spiral." *American Educator* (Fall). www.aft.org/ pubs-reports/american_educator/issues/fall04/reading.htm. Accessed June 18, 2005.

Towle, Wendy. 2000. "The Art of the Reading Workshop." *Educational Leadership* (September): 38–41.

Tucker, M. S., and Thomas Toch. 2004. "The Secret to Making NCLB Work? More Bureaucrats." *Phi Delta Kappan* 86 (1): 28–33.

Vang, Christopher. 2004. "Taking Scientific Approaches." *Language Magazine* 4 (4): 14–18.

Vygotsky, L. S. 1980. *The Mind and Society: The Development of Higher Psychological Processes.* Cambridge: Harvard University Press.

Willingham, Daniel T. 2004. "Practice Makes Perfect: But Only If You Practice Beyond the Point of Perfection." *American Educator* (Spring). www.aft.org/pubs-reports/american_educator/spring2004/ cogsci.html. Accessed June 18, 2005.

Winn, Ira J. 2004. "The High Cost of Uncritical Teaching." *Phi Delta Kappan* 85 (7): 496–97.

Winograd, Peter, Leila Flores-Dueñas, and Harriette Arrington. 2003. "Best Practices in Literacy Assessment." In *Best Practices in Literacy Instruction*, 2d ed., ed. Lesley Mandel Morrow, Linda B. Gambrell, and Michael Pressley, 201–37. New York: Guilford.

Wolfe, Patricia. 2001. *Brain Matters: Translating Research into Classroom Practice.* Alexandria, VA: Association for Supervision and Curriculum Development.

Wong Fillmore, Lily. 1999. Optimizing Conditions for Language and Learning in California: Beyond 227 and Beyond Y2K. California Elementary Association and Staff Development Resources Annual Conference, February 5, 1999. San Francisco.

Wong Fillmore, Lily, and Katherine E. Snow. 2000. *What Teachers Need to Know About Language.* ERIC document no. ED444379. Washington, DC: Center for Applied Linguistics.

Wren, Sebastian. 2000. *The Cognitive Foundations of Learning to Read: A Framework.* Austin, TX: Southwest Educational Development Laboratory.

Index

Meaning-making process, 70
Meaningful use, in conceptual teaching, 46–49
Mentor texts, studying, 69–70
Metacognitive strategies, in language workshop, 65
Middle school writing workshop, 7–8
Minilessons
    choosing, 90
    content-based. *See specific content-based lessons*
    on immigration, 98–106
    for language workshop, 55–57
    use of visuals in, 69
Modeling, for language learning, 9, 32, 101
Molly Lou Melon (Lovell), 40
Molly's Pilgrim (Cohen), 22–23
Motivation, for learning, 32
Mrs. Wishy-Washy (Cowley), 149–151
Music for Alice (Say), 148
My Cubing Inquiry (graphic organizer), 173
My Favorite Thing (According to Alberta) (Jenkins), 132
My Name is Maria Isabel (Ada), 39
The Mysterious Giant of Barletta (dePaola), 53–54

Narratives, units of study, 86
National Reading Panel, 50, 52
National standards
    essential learning goals from, 94–97
    in planning curriculum, 82
Native language, support/acceptance, 6
Natural approach, for second-language instruction, 61
Natural order hypothesis, for language acquisition, 28–29
Nettie's Trip South (Turner), 126
New-to-English students, books with simple language for, 183–184
No Child Left Behind Act of 2001, 17
Nonfiction
    conventions and information wall, 141
    summaries for, 140–142, 144
    units of study, 86
    visualization of, 143–145

Observation
    specific, on character traits, 152–153
    of struggling students, 25–26
Onomatopoeia, books with, 185
Organization, of units of study, 86

"Paired Squares Graphic" (graphic organizer), 152, 153, 164
Parenthetical explanations, 39
Passion, for teaching, 58–59
Peace and tolerance content-based lessons
    appreciating someone who thinks differently than you do, 114–116
    colors of peace and tolerance, 110–111
    differences and equality, 111–112
    how do you imagine peace, 106–110
    peace begins with tolerancey, 112–114
    text recommendations for read-alouds, 109
    unit-of-study design sheet, 107
Performance, student, 73, 74
Picture representations, of vocabulary words, 47–48, 148
Planning
    focus for, 82
    units of study, 88–90. *See also* Unit-of-study planning sheets
Plot, recognition of, 137–139
Plot line, 136–137
Poetry, units of study, 86
Point of reading, 155–156
Political contexts, of language teaching, 29–31
Practicing of English, 33, 48
Primary language, 9
Primary language instruction (bilingual programs), 30–31
Print, exposure to, 7
Problem solving, books on, 181–182
Process lessons, 21, 22, 61–63
Products, student, 73, 74, 85, 90
"Push/Pull Chart," 102, 103

Questions
    to clarify ideas, 153–155
    developing/encouraging, 69
    metacognitive, 71–72
    thick *vs.* thin, 118–120
Quick flashes of information, connections to, 130–132

Read-alouds. *See also under specific lessons*
    incidental word learning and, 52
    responding to, 109
    sharing ideas during, 109–110
    student discussions during, 101–102
    text recommendations for, 109

responsibilities during conferences, 75–76
student expectations of, 34
Teaching, language
focus, for vocabulary instruction, 36
focus for, 90
a language workshop, 4–5
order, *vs.* natural order of language acquisition, 28
passion for, 58–59
political contexts of, 29–31
resources, 84–85
sequence of. *See under specific minilessons*
strategies for English learners, 6, 56, 57
two prongs of. *See* Process lessons; Structure lessons
Text
clarifying ideas in. *See* Clarifying ideas in text
structure, 141
understanding, visualization and, 146–147
"Text Connections" (graphic organizer), 178
"Theme Analysis" (graphic organizer), 175
Thinking aloud, 108
Thinking wrap-up, 119–120
Tier one words, 50
Tier two words, 47, 50
Tier three words, 47, 50
Time factors, in language acquisition, 7
Tolerance, content-based language lessons on, 106–116
Touchstone text model, 101
Transformative teaching, 19–20
Triple T-chart, 148, 152
Two Bear Cubs: A Miwok Legend from California's Yosemite Valley (San Souci), 72

Understanding of reading selections, visualization and, 146–147
Unit-of-study planning sheets
blank, 91, 92
civil rights, 117, 123
clarifying ideas in text, 150
diversity, 123
lessons for all units, 93
on making connections/developing schemata, 127, 128, 129
on peace and tolerance, 107
synthesizing text through retelling, 134
on visualizing fiction and nonfiction, 143

Units of study, 83–87
advantages of, 84
content-based. *See* Content-based instruction
essential learning goals for, 94–97
features of, 87
focusing on, 83, 87
grade-level expectations and, 84
minilessons in. *See* Minilessons
planning, 88–90. *See also* Unit-of-study planning sheets
sample, 90, 93–94, 98–106
teaching resources for, 84–85

Venn diagrams, 45
Viewpoints, multiple, 124
Visualization, fiction/nonfiction
chart for, 145
focusing on mental images, 144–145
sensory images, 146
trying on a character, 148, 149
in understanding text, 146–147
unit-of-study planning sheet, 143
Visuals, 69. *See also* Graphic organizers
Vocabulary development, 35–52. *See also* Vocabulary instruction
for emotions, structured lesson on, 22–23
importance of, 35–36
incidental word learning through read-alouds, 52
reading development and, 36
support for, 38–39
through reading, 38–39
Vocabulary instruction, 36–40
charts, creating, 47–48, 49
choosing words for intensive instruction, 49–50
concept-based, 39–40
focus on, 49
framework for, 37
integration of, 43–45
introduction of words, 116, 118
lesson strategies, 44–45
linking with reading instruction, 50, 52
parts of, 37–38
picture representations of words, 47–48
schema theory and, 43–44
semantic maps for. *See* Semantic maps
teaching focus for, 36
Vocabulary-rich books, 38, 186–188

What Do You Know First (MacLachlan), 147–148
Whole-class sharing, 104, 111